D0600577

This Is the Sound!

The Best of Alternative Rock

by Randi Reisfeld

Aladdin Paperbacks

First Aladdin Paperbacks edition May 1996
Copyright © 1996 by Randi Reisfeld
Aladdin Paperbacks
An imprint of Simon & Schuster
Children's Publishing Division
1230 Avenue of the Americas
New York, NY 10020
The text of this book is set in 11-point Typewriter.
Printed and bound in the United States of America
10 9 8 7 6 5 4 3 2 1
Library of Congress Cataloging-in-Publication Data
Reisfeld, Randi.
    This is the sound : the best of alternative rock / by Randi Reisfeld.
       p. cm.
    Includes discographies.
    Summary: Identifies today's top alternative bands, observes what they're
saying, and points out how they're affecting the present generation.
ISBN 0-689-80670-1
1. Rock groups—Juvenile literature. 2. Rock music—History and criticism—Juvenile literature.
[1. Rock groups. 2. Musicians. 3. Rock music—History and criticism.] I. Title.
ML3929.R45 1996
781.66—dc20   95-43927

CONTENTS

Acknowledgments

The author gratefully thanks . . .

For tireless research, legwork, and facilitating: Janet Macoska

For sharing information and sources: Michael P. Shea, *Alternative Press* magazine; Marina Zogdi, *Metal Edge* magazine

For information, insights, and vital points of view: Scott Reisfeld, Stefanie Reisfeld, Lee Meyer, Lisa Alpern, Mindy Sonshine, Danny Mucciolo

For the idea: Julia Sibert, Aladdin Paperbacks

For support, understanding, love, and dinner: Marvin and Peabo

Introduction

Devout fans of alternative music rebuke the label. They're against pigeonholing and aghast that music journalists, who should know better, continue to do so. There's too much variety and too much substance within those musical and lyrical folds. Still, the music had to be called something, and in its infancy, it was an alternative to the mainstream of music that filled the airwaves and the glossy images on the MTV screen. For the growing generation that embraces it, alternative is music that invigorates, cuts close to the bone, stimulates the brain *and* the body, warms the soul, *and* touches the heart.

Alternative music is honest, and an honest reaction to the mindless, media-over-message music from such "stars" as Madonna and Bon Jovi. Instead, alternative music addresses the alienation and reflects the concerns, experiences, and fears of a new generation, playing an emotional sound track to their lives. It isn't, after all, a hap-hap-happy world out there: Alternative music reflects that reality. There are few silly love songs found in alt catalogues; instead, they dive into much deeper emotional waters, expressing powerful feelings of despair, lust, and confusion. In doing so, alternative music provides refuge, solace, and inspiration. It's music with a message and it's being heard and made all over the world.

The music that speaks to the vast population of echo-boomers (children of the '60s baby boomers) has roots that grew from two directions. From the east spawned the dreamy, poetic,  insightful R.E.M., led by Michael Stipe; while Seattle spewed forth the punky, angry, angst-ridden Nirvana, whose leader, the late Kurt Cobain, became alternative's first icon. Both seminal groups had powerful, poetic messages, both began on small, independent homegrown labels at a time when the majors had all but closed their doors—and ears—to anything new and different. The success of both groups kicked open the door for the stampede of new voices that followed.

Who listens to alternative? While fans are everywhere, they do share certain characteristics. More often than not, they're educated, introspective, sensitive. Alternative is music for today's thinking teenagers, collegiates, and those who may be older, but can still be touched by the turn of a lyric or moved by the crash of a guitar.

The purveyors of alternative music are becoming what they are: rock heroes and, for the first time in musical history, heroines. For there are just as many women rocking just as hard as the guys—and those who front many of these bands are on the forefront creatively; they're neither puppets nor window dressing, but the force behind the scenes and out front, too.

Who today's top alternative bands are, what they're saying, and how they're affecting this generation is what's in the pages of this book. This is the sound of today's music. A growing legion of talented musicians are making it: These are the bands who make it best.

THE WELL-CRAFTED—AND CRAFTY—VERSE OF ALTERNATIVE

Belly

7

PLAYERS

Tanya Donelly
vocals & guitar

Christopher Gorman
drums & percussion

Thomas Gorman
guitar & piano

Gail Greenwood
bass & vocals

King (Sire/Reprise) 1995
Star (Sire/Reprise) 1993

AWARDS & REWARDS

Grammy nominations: 1993 Best New Artist; 1994 Best Alternative Album
Star sold upwards of 800,000 copies in the U.S., achieving
Gold Record status; it reigned as the number one album on the college charts.
"Feed the Tree," *Star*'s stellar single, went to number 1.

Belly

ABOUT THEIR NAME

Belly was christened so by its leader, Tanya Donelly, simply because it's one of her favorite words. And because "it's pretty and ugly at the same time." That contradiction has been a metaphor for everything Belly ever since.

PRELUDE

They didn't set out to, but Boston-based Belly helped drop-kick alternative music squarely into the mainstream. At a time when few outside the college radio scene had heard of Tanya Donelly or Belly, the hooky/haunting "Feed the Tree" fed the airwaves and settled in the musical consciousness of the sing-along world. Didn't matter that the words weren't readily transparent—was "Take your hat off, boy, when you're talkin' to me" a retro feminist manifesto? Listeners were drawn into the song by the swirling rhythms, delivered in the lead singer's charged, yet baby-doll, voice, and the insistent beat. They stuck around to hear more.

More arrived in the form of Belly's no-less-oblique follow-up, "Gepetto"—metaphorically about Pinocchio's master—which proved that the group was no one-hit wonder. Belly was bulging with promise. *Star,* the CD that had spawned those singles, soared to the top of the college record charts and stayed for an amazing nine weeks. By the end of 1993, Belly was firmly implanted as "the cool new group of the '90s."

Of course, being "cool" had never been a priority of Belly's. Nor was "new" really part of the equation: The seeds of Belly had been planted long ago.

HERSTORY

Tanya Donelly is the high priestess—and "beast-ess," if you will—of this Belly. Without negating the crucial contributions of band mates Chris, Tom, and Gail, it is Tanya's poetically charged lyrics that have shaped the band; and her (yes) pop-friendly music that drives it still. Belly's story is Tanya's.

If biology is destiny, Tanya's might have been predicted by the time, place, and parentage into which she was born. The 1960s were in full kaleidoscopic throttle. It was a time of sharp societal divisions. There were those who fought hard to maintain the status quo, and those who fought just as hard against it. Tanya's folks were part of the free-flowing, free-loving rebellious scene; hippies who traveled among an irreverent crowd.

Tanya's earliest memories come from her first four years spent on the road with her parents. Unencumbered by structure or convention, her imagination ran vividly wild. "I remember little snatches of that trip," she says now. "I remember lilies of the valley in Arizona. I also had a lot of weird thoughts; I imagined I saw animals that couldn't have been there. At night we'd sleep outside sometimes, and my brother and I would sit there and make things up. 'There's a tiger outside the tent! There are gorillas standing on the fire escape! There are giraffes out in the hallway.'"

When she was four, her parents settled—in a fashion—in the trippy town of Newport, Rhode Island, an artists colony alive with creativity and all manner of music.

As a tiny tyke, Tanya was dressed for the part. "I looked like a little hippie with fringes and moccasins and ponchos and flowers in my hair," she recalls.

That may have been cool at home, but it was a no-go at school. When she got there, Tanya, who'd spent her life thus far among adults, was suddenly thrust among so many kids. "I was totally stressed out by it. I just wanted to be invisible," she remembers. It didn't help that she was immediately ostracized by her kiddie classmates for dressing different; being different. She reacted not by changing her style, but by vomiting. Her teachers reacted by sending Tanya to the back of the room. "It was fine by me," Tanya shrugs. "I wanted to be back there."

In spite of her problems at school, Tanya has rich memories of growing up. "I don't feel wounded by my childhood. I grew up loved and secure. I feel lucky to have been raised in an environment that allowed me the freedom to figure out what I wanted to do. My parents always listened, and left me alone to make my own decisions."

Among the defining moments of Tanya's childhood was meeting kindred spirit Kristin Hersh. The girls immediately entered into the time-honored contract of "best-friendship." If Kristin was the more outgoing one, the natural leader, she was also the more eccentric. The tinier and more earthbound Tanya hung back a bit. Still, they shared everything, including—a few years later, when Tanya's dad married Kristin's mom—parents and a bedroom.

As they got older, the now official stepsisters got more involved in music. They were influenced by some of the hard-edged '70s groups like the Pretenders and the Velvet Underground. Their common obsession, however, was the Beatles. "They were why I wanted a guitar," Tanya has said. Indeed, the girls didn't so much want to meet the band as be the band. So, they formed one. They were only acting naturally. As Tanya puts it, "Where we lived, everybody played an instrument. When I was a kid, you couldn't swing a dead cat without hitting a band."

Signing up for music lessons wasn't on the agenda; girls doing it for themselves was. With Beatles songbooks on their knees, Tanya and Kristin set out to teach themselves guitar and songwriting. "We started playing together and we did it from a real personal perspective," Tanya has explained. "We didn't know how to play, because we didn't listen to anybody else. So we kind of learned together. We thought the point was to be as interesting as possible and not to follow strict rules." That, of course, has made all the difference.

THROWING MUSES

The band they formed in 1981 was Throwing Muses. The girls were fifteen. Whether either Tanya or Kristin had the foresight to know it, Throwing Muses would far outlast their own teen years. Kristin was the undisputed star—the lead singer and most prolific songwriter. That was okay by Tanya, who wasn't emotionally, physically, or mentally ready to take charge. Being the guitar player was enough to fulfill her.

Armed with some original, edgy—though often imperceptible—songs, Throwing Muses began by touring local clubs around the northeast. True, their earliest gigs were often populated by parents and friends, but slowly their reputation grew and they became regular fixtures on the Boston-and-beyond club scene. Throwing Muses' success has historically been credited to Kristin: *her* songs, *her* haunting tremolo, *her* spellbinding presence onstage. The other members of the group were rarely, if ever, mentioned.

Although they'd eventually sign with a major U.S. record label (Sire/Reprise) in 1989, their first deal was with an independent in Britain called 4AD. A routine of writing songs, recording, and touring in support of the albums followed. With each successive offering, Throwing Muses got glowing reviews for albums of "delicate, surreal beauty." Commercial success, however, proved elusive. Tanya's contributions remained the same: onstage, she was the guitarist, offstage, the rule seemed to be that she could offer up to two tunes per album. But as the years went by, she was writing a whole lot more than that.

"The reason you start writing songs is because you're ugly and you're lonely and sitting in your room," Tanya has said. Did that signal her unhappiness with herself as part of Throwing Muses? That, Tanya has never said. But with the onset of the 1990s, she had an overload of original material. It was clear that most of it was never going to see the light of day if she stayed with Throwing Muses. So, after five albums and one EP, she didn't.

Because Tanya has mainly resisted talking about it, many have mused about why she really split—did she jump or was she pushed? Was she simply frustrated playing second-string to Kristin and not being able to record more of her own material? Did Kristin begin to regard Tanya as a threat? Or had Tanya always planned to split for her time in the spotlight? To the last rumination, Tanya has responded, "I wasn't in a band waiting for a time when I could make a solo record. I always considered myself the guitar player for Throwing Muses, until it got to the point where I had a bunch of songs. I didn't plan to break away until it became necessary."

That necessary departure caused a painful personal rift between the once inseparable stepsisters. For years afterward they barely spoke. What really happened, and why, only the two of them may ever know for sure. One clue may be in the final verse of "Judas My Heart," a song about betrayal: At the very end, Tanya alludes to the Beatles, her and Kristin's shared passion. The fab four said, "She loves you, yeah, yeah, yeah." Tanya's song ends with, "She loves me, yeah, yeah, yeah."

BECOMING BELLY
"My hands want to play pop songs and my head is attracted to despair." —Tanya Donelly

Before officially quitting Throwing Muses and forming her own band, Tanya took a couple of musical detours. She played briefly with an obscure outfit called This Mortal Coil. Better known is her tenure, from 1990–1992, with Kim Deal, formerly of the Pixies, in the Breeders. They released a relatively successful CD, *Pod*, as well as the EP *Safari*, but for Tanya, the Breeders became another breeding ground for what would soon grow into Belly.

In 1991, Tanya was contacted by a pair of hometown buddies, Christopher and Tom Gorman, most recently of local Providence band Verbal Assault. The brothers knew Tanya was flying solo and suggested teaming up to form a new group. Tanya "took it as a sign" and took not only the plunge, but full command. Now, she was ready. Dubbing her band Belly, she recruited former Muses bassist Fred Abong and hit the studio running. "We didn't really know what we were

doing," Tanya admitted later on. That didn't affect the finished product—or its shining success.

A few months later, *Star* was released. Nourished by its first single, "Feed the Tree," it exploded on alternative radio stations. More significantly, it answered the (pre-Green Day) question: Can authentic alternative have a strong pop sensibility without losing its edge? Can creative be commercial?

Tanya stood firm in her belief that she could make that seeming contradiction work, while acknowledging, "There is a certain strange shame that comes with being accepted and being palatable. But I never set out to be pop. It's just the music that comes out of me, the music I love." In the eyes of the "alt-police," being pop is equated with being disposable. And, of course, pop is the one form of music that alternative has always been an alternative *to*.

Belly became an anomaly on the alternative scene. *Star* soared to the top of several charts, including Muses territory (and far surpassing anything Kristin's band ever did): the college/alternative charts. Indeed, Belly blew open the door for more pop-oriented alternative bands who followed, such as Green Day and the cranberries.

Fans weren't the only ones who noticed. Reviewers jumped on the Belly bandwagon, proclaiming *Star*, "A bristling, beautiful record that mixes inviting hooks, melodies and choruses of probing lyrics." Pundits pounced, too, on Tanya's effervescent talent. "With her clear and hesitant voice, she scatters surrealistic snapshots over jangly and jagged guitars," noted *Spin* magazine.

If *Star* twinkled brightly with pop songs and sparkling promise, Belly's sophomore effort, *King*, released in 1995, was nothing less than regal. More of a collaborative effort than *Star*, *King* featured the co-songwriting talents of Chris, Tom, and the band's newest recruit, bassist Gail Greenwood, a refugee from a hard-edged Newport, Rhode

Island, band called the Dames.

More dominant musically and lyrically and even *more* pop-accessible, *King,* without the benefit of a penetrating standout single, got universally glowing reviews. "*King* is suffused with effortlessly catchy songs and endlessly quirky twists," they raved. "Tanya's lyrics are startlingly intimate and head-scratchingly oblique."

And Now, a Word (or Several) about Those Lyrics

It has become a game—an obsession, really—among Belly-heads to try to figure out what-all Tanya is writing about. (Not all fans of alternative music particularly care what songs are *about.* It seems most Belly fans—who Tanya herself has affectionately dubbed "wounded nerds everywhere"—do, however.) Are the songs absolutely autobiographical? She says emphatically no. Tanya bristles: "I don't want my songs to become like barf bags for my psyche (are you listening, Eddie Vedder?); I'm not really interested in that kind of public display. There are things that come out, but they are not special to me. I try to keep it in that context."

So did she just make everything up? Are her lyrics just so much poetic free association? Try again. Belly songs are not written to confuse. Each is carefully crafted and well thought out about the effect it may have on listeners. "If you're gonna write something that sticks in somebody's head, you always have to

be real careful about what that's gonna mean. If it's gonna be something that runs through someone's head, it had better be worth it," says the songwriter sagely.

What that something is, however, she's not saying. In other words, *there is no definitive answer.* At least not one Tanya's ready to cop to. Even her bandmates are left twisting in the wind, as Gail attests: "Sometimes I'll ask her, point-blank, 'Is this about so-and-so?' And sometimes, she'll say, 'It could be,' and other times, she'll say, 'I'm not telling.'"

What *can* be said about Belly music is this: Some songs are bizarrely enigmatic while snatches, at least, of others seem painfully clear. Some songs probably *are* autobiographical, while others are pulled from some distant imaginative galaxy.

More often than not, Belly songs contain the contradiction that defines the band. Beautiful images, lilting melodies, juxtaposed with disturbing, scary lyrics. The same word used as a verb and then again as a noun, with opposing meanings. On purpose. Explains Tanya, "I'm always interested in dichotomy and paradox, the kind of things . . . that trick you. Really morbid pop has always attracted me. Something that seems sweet, but ends up burning you." Just when you think the song is about one thing, it takes a sharp turn and turns out to be about something else entirely.

It's like how Tanya described her attraction to the word *belly* in the first place: "pretty and ugly at the same time."

That said, it's fascinating to see the spin some have put on specific songs compared to what Tanya herself has said about them (whether she's being truthful or not is also open to interpretation) and with what is known about her.

"FEED THE TREE"

Powered by a driving lead guitar, "Feed the Tree" is an accessible toe-tapper with rhythms that seem to swirl and spin round and round. Delivered in Tanya's breathy, sometimes hesitant, then more assured voice, it evokes images perhaps of a young girl in a flowing dress spinning circles around a tree. But the words contradict any carefree, childlike image.

At first listen to the insistent hook—"Take your hat off, boy, when you're talkin' to me"—it might seem to be some sort of retro feminist manifesto. But (to paraphrase the song itself) we know all this and more: "Feed the tree" is an old New England expression referring to a tradition about death. It is said that when a person dies and is buried in the ground, a tree should be planted directly above so the roots grow into the body, allowing the corpse to feed the tree and give it life. We also know, because she's admitted it, that Tanya suffered a near-death experience in a car accident and used to be obsessed with the hereafter. "I got superstitious. . . . I saw signs that meant imminent death in everything."

Several listens later, themes of respect for the wisdom of elders, life cycles, death, burial, and the sanctity of the grave seem to emerge. Maybe. Or maybe Tanya's just taking on the persona of a wise old man ("this old man I've talked about/used to be") passing down his wisdom to a reckless, feckless (and now toothless, as an old man might be) child.

"KING"

The title track from Belly's second album contains powerful, starkly unsettling images. The most common interpretation has the song clearly about child abuse and incest, about a father-as-predator preying on a trusting child who sees him as an all-powerful faith healer, but also as a faithless companion. Indeed, a read of the lyrics seems to make this one of Belly's most transparent and jarring songs. Seems to. Perhaps the most jarring thing about "King," then, is reading Tanya's take on it. She told a British fanzine that "King" was dedicated to a friend's lighting technician brother, who was hired by a prince to brighten up his birthday party with lights—so he lit up the ocean bed. Tanya equated the image of a dark and dangerous ocean being changed into something bright and beautiful with a kind of love. "As soon as you're in love, you're in incredible danger," she is quoted. "You're floating on top of this ocean with things underneath that can kill you; how wonderful and terrifying that is! In the middle of this fear, you have these lights, and this wonderful naked person you can go home to." And "King," she explained, is just another way of saying "Roi," the person's name (Roy)—and also the name of a Breeders' tune.

Belly songs may all be fair game for interpretation, but that doesn't mean Tanya is playing games—with her songs, or her fans' heads. Call it what you will, it's all right with Tanya. In fact, it's the way she wants it: "All the songs are about something, but they're not literal. I want people to put themselves into the song. That's what I do when I listen to R.E.M. I don't really care what Michael's [Stipe] story is, I just appropriate it for my own." Take what you will from Belly: It's what it's there for.

BELLY BUTTONS

◊ Tanya will always be connected to Kristin Hersh and Kim Deal personally. The rift with Kristin has healed, and Tanya allows, "Kristin will always have a foremost seat on the jury of my life." She remains close with the Breeders' Kim Deal, and with Kim's sister Kelley, who replaced Tanya in that band.

◊ Belly and Juliana Hatfield share the same manager, Gary Smith.

◊ Gary heads Boston's Fort Apache Studios, home to Juliana and the Lemonheads.

◊ Gary's grandfather is Chris Gorman's landlord.

◊ Chris shot the album cover art for *King*.

◊ Tanya's birthday is July 14, 1966.

◊ Tanya never did learn to read music. She's still unaware of the names of the chords she's playing. "I hear the sound of the song in my head and I have to make the guitar do that thing."

◊ Tanya thinks it's weird that people aren't embarrassed to talk about negative things, but are embarrassed to talk about God.

◊ Tanya still gets nervous just before going onstage.

◊ What Everyone Says about Tanya: She's nice.

◊ Where to Write: Belly, c/o Fort Apache, One Camp Street, Suite 2, Cambridge, MA 02140.

the cranberries

THE SWEET-TART OF ALTERNATIVE

CRANBERRIES

Dolores O'Riordan
lead singer, song-writer, acoustic guitars, keyboards

Noel Hogan
electric & acoustic guitars

Mike Hogan
bass guitar

Feargal Lawler
drums & percussion

No Need to Argue (Island) 1994

Everybody Else Is Doing It,
So Why Can't We? (Island/PLG) 1993

Uncertain (Xeric) 1991

21

AWARDS & REWARDS

Everybody Else Is Doing It has sold three and a half million copies so far; it is still charting.
No Need to Argue has topped four million sales units; its peak position on the American pop charts was number 9.
Won Best Irish Recording Artists at the 1995 World Music Awards.
Named Best Irish Act at the 10th Annual Irish Music Awards.

the cranberries

ABOUT THEIR NAME

BD: Before Dolores, they were known as The Cranberry Saw Us—which, uttered quickly, sounded like the bad pun intended, "The Cranberry Sauce." It was chosen simply because "It came up in conversation one day." A silly reason for a silly name for what was then a not-very-serious band.

AD: After Dolores, they got down to business and became the cranberries: lowercase intentional, because (they say) "we like being humble."

OVERTURE

The cranberries are Ireland's most successful export since U2 and Sinead O'Connor. They are often—and not unfairly—compared to both. Like the former, the cranberries can strike a tart political chord (witness "Zombie" and "The Icicle Melts"); like the latter, they hit the high notes of bittersweet personal tragedies and triumphs (listen to "Linger" and "Dreaming My Dreams") with equal fervor. Of import, the cranberries—via only two albums—are most responsible for spreading the appeal of alternative music all over the world. Turn to any Top 10 chart in any country—from their native Ireland to Italy or Indonesia—and there's likely to be a cranberries sampling. The cranberries have proven that when the musical message gets to the heart of the matter, it hits home(s) all over the world. It all has to do with human emotions and human feelings.

Of course, it isn't just the message, it's the messenger—and the cranberries deliver one of the most distinct, in the dulcet tones of lead singer Dolores O'Riordan. It's her enchanting, octave-leaping voice out front, and once heard, it can neither be forgotten nor ignored. It is she who is most responsible for powering the band to international acclaim. It's a bit ironic, then, that for all their worldly success, the cranberries themselves are anything but. Their roots are resolutely small town.

CRANBERRY SEEDLINGS

The seeds of what would eventually be the cranberries were nurtured in the small coastal city of Limerick, Ireland. The band was officially formed in 1990 by teenage guitar-playing brothers Noel and Mike Hogan and drummer-pal Feargal Lawler. It featured a fellow named Niall on lead vocals who also composed the ditties. The combo seemed to take its musical cue from the name of their hometown—a limerick, of course, being a type of silly, irreverent, nonsensical verse. Not only did the band sport a suitably jokey name, The Cranberry Saw Us, they sowed their silly oats in their often-as-not nonsensical music. A sample of their lyrics went: "Throw me down a big stairs; I want to bleed on a brand-new carpet." Later on, Dolores would dismiss

it as "music by a load of teenage boys having fun after school."

Maybe so, but these particular teenage boys actually had quite a bit more depth of feeling than their earliest melodies might suggest. It was lighthearted; the musicians (with the exception of Niall) were not. For the Hogan brothers and Feargal had taken their fair share of youthful lumps. Because they were not students, they'd grown up feeling like outsiders in their own community. "If you weren't chasing a university degree, you were looked down on," they allege of life in Limerick. "If you're not interested in academics, you're a piece of scum . . . worthless."

With feelings like those, it's not surprising that their goofy age was short-lived. By 1991, Niall had departed for a new band, and instrumentalists Noel, Mike, and Feargal decided on a change of course; something—or someone—to encapsulate the spirit of the prettier, lusher, more thoughtful tunes they'd been quietly turning out. While they weren't looking specifically for a girl, there was someone, unbeknownst to them, sprouting up just a few miles down the country road whose path was about to cross theirs. And she would make all the difference.

Dolores O'Riordan grew up the youngest

in a family of seven children—all boys with the exception of herself and a sister. Money was never in huge supply as Dolores' dad had been disabled in a motorcycle accident and her mom worked as a caterer to support the large clan. By Dolores' account, self-worth for girls was something else in short supply. "My mom always had a softer spot for the boys, a lot of Irish women do. Boys could just sit there and be brilliant, just for being boys. If you were a girl [to get positive attention], you'd have to wear a pretty dress, or sing." Tomboy Dolores never was much for dresses, pretty or otherwise; so singing it was, and singing she did. She possessed the natural ability and always had *that* voice: It brought the spotlight on her.

She sang at school—an Irish national school where many subjects were taught in traditional Gaelic—and the teachers used that voice to corral unruly students into attentiveness. "If I started to sing, all the others in the room would stop and listen," Dolores testifies.

She sang in church, "in liturgical choirs, very soft, not as boisterous as the Irish folk music." She was elevated to choir soloist.

She sang in pubs, when she was still very small. "I'd go and sing country-and-western songs," she remembers.

She entered countywide and then national singing competitions and, often as not, came home with the prize.

She came to believe that she was born to sing. "Since I was a child I've believed that the reason why I've been put on earth has been to sing and deliver a message . . . I've always felt it."

She learned her first instrument, the tin whistle, when she was five. "It's like learning to speak when you're a kid, in certain schools in Ireland you learn how to play the whistle and you can play it with your eyes closed, hanging upside down." Later, she took classical piano lessons and mastered the keyboards.

And she began writing her first songs. "I started writing as a diversion," she admits, "but I was very serious about what I wrote." As a teenager, she wrote what she knew. "Most of my songs were about myself. I grew up with a lot of guys. I felt like I was one of them. Then I realized I wasn't. I got into relationships and it was weird. I wanted love straightaway, but if I showed affection, they ran away. I had a horrible experience with every one of them. Guys would just break my heart. I couldn't say things straight to them, so I wrote them down." The first song she ever wrote was "Calling." It was about a twelve-year-old girl with an unrequited crush on a much older man.

Twelve-year-old Dolores listened to the king, Elvis himself—she related to his humble rural roots—and the traditional American country tunes of Patsy Cline. Later, she'd go for Duran Duran, Spandau Ballet, and Depeche Mode. All of them influenced her, but none from the vantage point of a first-row seat, or even the balcony. Dolores did not go to concerts. She quipped, "The first gig I went to was my own."

A career in music might have been a "ridiculous thought" were it not for all those church- and school-sponsored competitions years back. "If it hadn't been for church, I wouldn't have thought of music as a career in the first place. Of course I love singing. It's what I always wanted to do, but I never thought it would really happen." No Irish woman she knew had gone into the modern music world—except, later on, Sinead O'Connor. While Dolores doesn't exactly acknowledge the controversial singer as a role model, she does nod to the influence. "For an Irish woman to get up and sing rock 'n' roll made me want to do it."

It didn't make her parents want her to do it, however. Much as the desire to join a band was growing, Dolores did not have their support. "I wasn't allowed to join a rock band until I'd finished school." To her parents' chagrin, she first heard about The Cranberries' search for a singer right there at school. One of her classmates knew someone who knew of the opening.

The audition was not a one–sided affair. She was sizing up Noel, Mike, and Feargal as much as they were listening to her offerings. She was the tougher to convince, less impressed with their material than their potential. Dolores recalls, "They were doing funny stuff with stupid titles like 'My Granny Drowned in a Fountain at Lourdes.' But I thought what they were playing was very nice. I liked the music, which had something about it."

As for Noel, Mike, and Feargal, their trepidations had more to do with Dolores' roots—here was this fresh, sweet girl coming in from the country, after all— than her pipes. Which didn't surprise her. She knew that the boys were going to be impressed "the minute I opened my mouth." She was right. "After they heard me sing, we got on famously." Little did they know how famous they'd become, and how fast.

RIPE FOR THE PICKING
"We expected a good reaction, but we thought it would take longer to happen, maybe two or three years." —Feargal Lawler

Because the cranberries hit it big so quickly, it's tempting to think it was all handed to them—recording contract, garnished with gold records, generously sprinkled with acclaim—on a silver platter. And, in rock terms, things did happen swiftly for them, but they weren't dining on caviar and champagne from the get-go. There was some bitter fruit to taste before the cranberries ripened on the vine.

Still, within three weeks of Dolores' audition, the renamed band—officially now, the cranberries—was in a local Limerick studio called Xeric recording its first demos. Their first cassette-only single was called "Nothing Left at All."

The band began to draw attention locally, playing in whatever dumps and dives would have them. Their first gig was in a hotel basement in Limerick. It was October, 1990, and a grand total of sixty people were in attendance. The musicians were terrified. "It was a really small, dark room," Feargal recalled to *Rolling Stone*. "We just went up and we had six songs. Dolores was turned to the side; Noel, Mike, and I had our heads down. [In fact, Feargal would cover his face with his cymbals.] It went from, 'No! There's no audience out there, please turn the lights off in my face,' to, 'OK, let's get this over with, and that'll be it.'"

The onstage bashfulness didn't seem to hurt. For on the strength of their demo—which was being passed around and played on radio stations—the British and Irish music press quickly glommed onto the band, canonizing the shy gang of four as "the next big thing." The tower of babble was as flattering as it was unexpected, but it wasn't paying the rent.

And those were lean times. "We made no money, we got 15 pounds (the equivalent of about $25) a day, which goes nowhere in Europe." Yet they soldiered on.

They traveled by van in spaces so tight that Dolores often slept draped across the boys' laps. Many a night, they'd crash on people's floors. "It's just not nice," commented Dolores. Bad luck stalked them. "We used to stand there, very still, and things always went wrong. Things exploded all the time." And to top it off, live, they weren't very good. They wouldn't get more comfortable, or better, for a long time.

They learned to adapt. When they were hungry, they leeched off the headlining band's food. "We'd steal their sandwiches after the gig—free food," they can now shamelessly admit.

Looking back, the cranberries say that in spite of it all, they're actually grateful to have started with nothing. As expressed by Feargal, "We could really appreciate it when it got better."

It got better quickly.

Every band hopes for a record contract: It's the pot of gold at the end of the rainbow, and the cranberries were no different. Despite the hype in the press, they knew the odds were against them. Still, they gamely kept at it, recording more demos. Noel would sit at home and diligently send copies of those demos out to record labels and radio stations. "I spent every day, from morning till teatime, writing out labels and ringing people up," he describes.

Neither Noel nor anyone else in the band expected much from their efforts; after all, every hard-luck music story they'd ever heard was about how long it took to get someone, anyone, interested. Clearly, the cranberries had something the others didn't: They got lots of someones interested. Record company responses began to trickle, then pour in. But each wanted to see them perform live. With much trepidation, the cranberries played a showcase at a local university. To their shock, an actual bidding war between major labels ensued.

In 1992, Island Records won the battle, and the cranberries set to work on their debut album.

Nothing went smoothly. Produced at first by Pearse Gilmore, owner of the recording studio and the band's original manager, the rough cuts of the album did not reflect the cranberries' music. Gilmore had cluttered it with dance beats and industrial-style guitar. Worse than screwing up their music, the band realized that their manager had been screwing them, telling Noel one thing, Dolores something else, and Feargal yet something else entirely. Money was missing.

In the end, the cranberries had to rid themselves of the manager, the early tracks of their album, and the bad vibes. What didn't break them up, though, toughened them up. "When we fired our manager, it made us stronger," recounts Dolores. "I knew I would never again let anyone make me do something I didn't want to do, or tell me what to do." It also led to a burst of creativity. "When we broke up with our manager, everybody was feeling the same kind of emotion, and all that music just came out."

All that music is what went on their first album, *Everybody's Doing It, So Why Can't We?* The name was a nod to their new confidence. They may have been uncertain onstage, but they knew they had the chops in the grooves. "There's loads of other bands that just can't sing out there making records ," declared Dolores. "We're 20 times better than them."

At first blush, it seemed few agreed with them. For the British music press, who'd been heaping praise upon the unsigned band, suddenly had a change of heart when the album finally came out. *Everybody's Doing It*—with its strong, subtle, swirling melodies and gorgeous sound scapes—was inexplicably panned in the cranberries' homeland.

Noel, Mike, Feargal, and Dolores were surprised—and hurt. For they had no previous experience with a music press that loves to knock down whoever it has previously built up. The Brits—never at a loss for a jab—pounced on their shyness, dubbing Dolores "The Girl Who Stands Sideways" for her initial reluctance to face her audience.

"We were teenagers when it all started, just doing music because we wanted to, and then things happened so fast. One minute we were rehearsing at home, and the next we were plastered on every paper. It takes awhile to get used to it, to be able to cope with it," Feargal has commented.

What eventually helped them not only cope, but thrive, was experience, a thickening of their emotional skins—and the U.S.A. It was there, not as a pop or rock act, but on the alternative music charts, where the cranberries gained real, lasting acceptance, as well as exceptional reviews and stellar sales. Which forced the British to re-evaluate their anti-'berries stand. With kinder reviews at home, sales of the cranberries' album eventually soared.

The embracement by the American alternative scene did wonders for their self-image as well; the cranberries' music from then on would reflect it.

EVERYBODY'S DOING IT, SO WHY CAN'T WE?

"Our music comes from inside, it's a little magic between the four of us." —Dolores O'Riordan

The cranberries' music is to be listened to, ingested and savored; it's music that's meant to "linger" in the brain and the heart. It's quiet, almost polite, for Dolores has no need to shout. There is power enough in its captivating simplicity.

The real power, many would argue, is Dolores' voice. Her octave-leaping range is nothing short of rapturous. She delivers her dirges in her clipped Celtic howls and weepy cries. As *Pulse!* magazine put it, "She can bellow like a bullhorn ("Zombie") or trip delicately through a quiet, meadowy waltz, as in 'Dreaming My Dreams.'" Dolores' voice is nothing less than its own instrument, one of unspoiled beauty. It swoops and quavers with quiet insistence.

Although Dolores insists that "the lads"—Noel, Feargal, and Mike—have final approval over the cranberries' material, most of what the world hears is from their lead singer's fertile pen and open heart. Their music is Dolores' music. It has changed as she, and her outlook, have grown.

The songs are easy to understand—easily heartfelt and gripping. They are about loss, longing, and redemption. Indeed, there's virtually no ambiguity in cranberry lyrics. As opposed to her peers, Dolores wants her songs interpreted *as she meant them:* She has little interest in listeners co-opting the music to suit themselves. "I've decided to write for myself, to write from personal experience," she states. "I write about what is getting to me at the time, about things you need to talk about but that would sound silly if you sat down and told them to your friend." And to make sure they're taken as intended, Dolores inks liner notes beneath the lyrics for further explanation. "Zombie," she states (for those who might've missed the point) is about "man's inhumanity to man, and worse still, to children." And "Disappointment" was "written on making a clear decision; no more struggle inside."

The tracks on *Everybody's Doing It* autobiographically reflect Dolores' earliest romantic experiences. It's a sepia-toned album full of somber breakup songs. It is also filled with traditional Celtic vibes; Dolores' deeply Irish churchgoing roots are obvious. Indeed, "Alosa," dedicated to Dolores' departed grandfather, is Celtic for "Jesus."

The heartbreak songs are what stand out, though.

The dreamy, string-powered "Linger"—the first song the group wrote together—became one of their signature songs as well as an MTV staple. It is about the kind of loss one never gets over—the loss of a first love, in her case, a seventeen-year-old soldier who shipped out.

"It evolved out of two kisses and a slow dance at the disco," Dolores reveals. "Most of it happened inside my head—sometimes I can get very dramatic about these things."

The jagged, vibratoed "Dreams," another of the band's early hits, was a sublimely rousing, though angst-ridden teenager-in-love song. "Oh my life is changing, every day in every possible way," was its simplistic message. As delivered by Dolores, though, there are knots and twists and gasps in every syllable: "Dreams" hypnotizes.

NO NEED TO ARGUE

"We don't write songs like 'I love you, I love you, let's get married.' Our topics are varied—social, personal, family, just about so many different things. They're not stupid."
—Dolores O'Riordan

Just two years after their debut, the cranberries delivered their second album. While it was driven by the lush, ethereal waves of sound they're famous for, lyrically—and sometimes musically—it was a marked departure from the first. If most of *Everybody's Doing It* was sweet, the 'berries bared their tart side on *No Need to Argue*. It was, by any measure, stronger, angrier, and in its way, more poignant than the first.

The industrial strength "Zombie" was the bridge song between the two albums. Written during the tour in support of *Everybody's Doing It* (and performed during it), "Zombie" signaled a broadening of their musical horizons. It was their most powerful song, written not about one person's lost love, but of many lost to the viciousness of war. "Zombie" is about the well-chronicled troubles in

Northern Ireland: It is an indictment of the "tanks and the bombs and the guns," a plea to stop the fighting, and above all, an elegy for a child killed in the war.

"Zombie," which pulsates with anger at the stupidity and waste of violence done in the name of politics and religion, has become the cranberries' new signature song. It also proved the cranberries' diversity.

Think again if you thought they could only do sweet, quiet, and lush. This group can clearly handle aggression and anger.

This delights Dolores, who has attested, "It's a growing thing. We have evolved and we've more confidence. I became more experimental. On the first album the songs were acoustic based. On the second, I wanted "Zombie" to be a really aggressive song because it was about an aggressive subject: a child's life being taken by violence. I wrote the lyrics on my guitar and told the band, 'I want this to sound really heavy, really aggressive. It's not about falling in love. . . . It's an angry song.'"

And just in case "Zombie" was misinterpreted, the video spelled it out: in black, white, silver, and gold. Screaming children are painted in silver; Dolores' image is covered in gold. "Silver and gold symbolize the beauty that we see in our world, or that we care to open our eyes to. The screaming and the cross and the real black-and-white footage symbolize the pain that's there and we close our eyes to: the children that suffer and the parents and families that suffer," she explained.

The raging images and those of soldiers patroling Belfast's streets did not go unnoticed: An ensuing controversy resulted in "Zombie"'s ban from Radio One in England on the grounds that it was too harsh.

The tormented "The Icicle Melts" carried the theme further—perhaps even further than intended. "I don't know what's happening to people today, when a child is taken away," Dolores mourns. While it was written again about innocent children lost in Belfast bombings, it could just as easily refer to the babies blasted away in Oklahoma. Or in Israel, Lebanon, or Bosnia—"anywhere in the world innocents are slaughtered in the name of politics."

There's no dearth of the lush melodies cranberries fans crave: Listen to the dreamily intoxicating "Ode to My Family." The album's first cut, which is, in fact, the deepest, is about Dolores' sudden success and subsequent yearning to return to her simple childhood. "We were raised to see life as fun and take it if we can," is the oft-repeated chorus.

And then there's "Dreaming My Dreams"—Dolores' first full-tilt love-gone-right song. Unabashedly romantic, it is dedicated to her husband, lover, best friend, support: Don Burton. It's her love-at-long-last waltz—the kind of song that might well be played for a first (or last—"What more can be said?" she asks in the liner notes) dance at a wedding.

From the anger of loss to the sweet fulfillment of love, *No Need to Argue* had it all. No one is arguing with its success—in "Ode to My Family," Dolores wonders aloud, "Does anyone care?" Millions did. The cranberries' sophomore effort has sold over five million records, and is still going strong.

FRESH-SQUEEZED CRANBERRIES

What lies ahead for "those nice little cranberries from Ireland" is certainly more juice, lyrically, musically and in the flesh. For the 'berries refuse to be preserved in just one tight-lidded jar—they're confident and feeling their oats. "If I wanted to do a jazz song, we could do it tomorrow . . . or a metal song," Dolores attests. There are, in fact, some songs they've already done that point the way to what fans can expect on their third album.

Clearly, they won't stop protesting war's insanity. "War Child," done with stark, acoustic guitar, is already being performed in concert. So is "I Just Shot John Lennon," an ode to a fallen hero, "about how somebody so brilliant can be terminated so quickly by somebody so irrelevant."

Performing live is an area the band hopes to improve on. "I want to build on our live following," declares Dolores. "When people come back after the show and say, 'Oh, that was a great gig,' or, 'You made me cry,' I feel really happy."

So there are plans, but there are also contingency plans as well. "Life is so unpredictable that there's no point in planning anything," laments Dolores. "There's a line in 'Empty' that goes, 'All my plans fell through my hands.' None of us takes things too seriously and if it all ended tomorrow, we'd just think, 'All well and good, we had a good time.'"

DOLORES DOES DECLARE . . .

Though much of her music has been described as quiet and polite, her prose is anything but. And yes, it has gotten her into a bit of hot water now and again. Herewith, a sampling of some of her spicier bits.

ON WOMEN:

"I couldn't work with women. I reckon I'd kill 'em. Too many women together and we'd get on each other's nerves."

ON CERTAIN WOMEN:

"Janet Jackson and Mariah Carey are marketing projects. They're not real artists at all. Janet Jackson can't sing; her songs are all the same. . . ."

ON HER IMAGE:

"I don't like [using one's sexuality] as a selling point. I don't like that to be a priority. It wasn't my sexuality that got me where I am today. I don't need to capitalize on my body because I'm selling songs and lyrics."

ON THE PRESS:

"None of those writers has a clue as to who I am—they just get a look at the visual."

ON CONCERTS:

"I don't like to go see bands. I get a headache. I don't know how people come to see us."

ON RECORDING:

"I like to record in the dark, because your mind wanders a bit more when there's nothing to look at. Your imagination is freer, there's nobody intimidating you. You can drift into what you're singing about more."

ON SUCCESS:

"It's not important to make the Top 10—it's important to be respected as really good musicians."

Where to Write:

THE CRANBERRIES, c/o Island Records, 400 Lafayette Street, New York, NY 10003.

THE POP-PUNK OF
Green Day
ALTERNATIVE

MEMBERS

BILLIE JOE ARMSTRONG
lead singer &
guitar player

Mike Dirnt
bass
guitar

Tré Cool
drums

CDs

Insomniac (Warner/Reprise) 1995

Dookie (Warner/Reprise) 1994

Kerplunk (Lookout Records) 1992

1,039/Smoothed Out Slappy Hours (Lookout Records) 1990

Green Day

HOW THEY GOT THEIR NAME

Used to be, every day was a "green" day for Billie, Mike, and Tré, i.e., one spent hanging out and smoking marijuana. But it wasn't always their name. Back in 1987, they were Sweet Children. Two years later they changed it to Green Day, lifted from a tune—their ode to hanging out and smoking—on their first album, *1,039/Smoothed Out Slappy Hours*.

These days are greener than ever for the trio: Only now, the color no longer refers to reefer, but money. Green Day is piling up the greenbacks. With good cause.

PREAMBLE
"I never really thought that being obnoxious would get me to where I am now."
—Billie Joe Armstrong

It would be easy to dismiss Green Day as a bunch of obnoxious punks who are getting paid (really well) for being incorrigible. The insurgent trio, after all, pour a lot of energy into fueling their bad boy image: playing concerts in the nude, hurling obscenities at each other and at their audience, just saying "yes" to all the things we've been warned to "just say no" to.

Their music plays to the image. No Green Day song overstays its welcome. All short and cynical, an entire album of fourteen songs runs thirty-nine minutes. No song is too obscure; all revolve around themes every adolescent can relate to: isolation, frustration, the opposite sex, boredom with the present, fear of the future. No song is overly orchestrated; all are executed with one blasting guitar, a bass, and three drum chords.

What else could be expected, after all, of a group named after an illegal substance, who titled their multi-platinum album with a slang word for *excrement*? It all seems to fit, all too well.

But all is not what it seems. For Green Day could not have gotten where it has, enveloped in a smoke-filled haze. Dig beneath the dookie and you find three serious—and, yes, seriously talented—musicians who have paid their dues, professionally and personally. You find a trio so tenacious, they'd do—make that, they *did*—anything and everything to make it.

GREEN ROOTS

Green Day's roots are found in the arid soil of Rodeo, not to be confused with the tony Rodeo Drive of Beverly Hills. This is what can kindly be called a working-class suburb of Berkeley, California. It's home to both Billie Joe Armstrong and Mike Dirnt.

Billie Joe is the son of a jazz musician who worked as a truck driver. Money was never plentiful, but in the beginning at least, music was. The whole family sang and played instruments. Billie, the youngest of six, was the prodigy. He could carry a tune by the age of two. So pure was his voice that by five, he was traveling the county to sing at nursing homes and children's hospitals. He taught himself guitar and composed his first rudimentary songs well before high school.

But Billie was never exactly the model son. He hated authority, and his natural bent toward rebellion was exacerbated by his dad's death and the subsequent shattering of his family. His mother waitressed to support the clan and later remarried a man her children disliked.

"There was a lot of physical fighting," Billie has said.

Billie was ten at the time—and just about to form the most important relationship of his life. That's when he met Mike.

Mike's path was rougher by a country mile. Born Michael Pritchard to a heroin-addicted mother, he was adopted by a biracial couple who divorced when Mike was seven. Although he bounced between them, his strongest parental relationship was with neither, but with the man who eventually became his stepdad. "He instilled a lot of blue-collar values in me," Mike has said by way of tribute. Unfortunately, that connection was severed when the man died. Mike was seventeen. He had it no easier in school. Diagnosed as hyperactive, he was often the target of cruel taunting by the other kids.

One who didn't taunt him was Billie Joe Armstrong. The boys formed a friendship bonded by music, a commodity hard to come by in Rodeo, where no stores stocked records. The friends had to travel to Berkeley to look at albums. "If you wanted to hear music, you had to play it," Mike said. Billie picked up a cheap Stratocaster guitar, Mike did likewise, and the self-professed "eleven-year-old geeks" began playing together. Inspiration was found on the radio in the form of the Clash, the Sex Pistols, and the Kinks, and later on, the Replacements and Operation Ivy. The music emanating from the crunching dual guitars of Billie and Mike was "our version of bad heavy metal." Sometimes they played covers of other people's songs; sometimes they tried performing Billie's originals. Even in those early days, the songs Billie wrote weren't appreciably different than they are today: He wrote about what he knew, the pain and joy of being a teenager, and set it to a breakneck beat.

In 1987, Billie and Mike formed their first "official" band. Perversely, they named themselves Sweet Children and over the next few years, along with a succession of drummers including Al Sobrante and John Kiftmeyer, played anywhere and everywhere they could. Nothing was beneath them: school dances, backyard parties, the tiniest and grungiest of clubs. "I wouldn't call it work," Billie laughs, "'cause we didn't get paid." They also didn't get respect. One unexceptional night, while playing the lounge of a roadside café, Billie's mother called in the middle of their set— admonishing him to come home and finish his chores.

Meanwhile, in the mountains of Mendocino, California, a youngster who'd eventually call himself Tré Cool was growing up isolated, lonely, *très* uncool. "It was mind-numbing," Tré has said of his rural roots. "I'd walk around this huge mountain; it was complete wilderness." The boy, then known as Frank Edwin Wright III, the son of a Vietnam veteran, began his musical training early on, learning to play violin in second grade.

Tré's house was so isolated that his nearest neighbor was miles away: Lucky not only for him, but for all of what would become Green Day, that the neighbor happened to be Lawrence Livermore, leader of a punk rock group and founder of an independent record label.

When Livermore's group, the Lookouts, needed a drummer, he recruited his then twelve-year-old neighbor and rechristened him Tré Cool. Though Tré's tenure with the Lookouts didn't last very long, the association with Lawrence Livermore did. It would prove serendipitous.

Back in Berkeley, Sweet Children were evolving into a tighter unit. Mike had taken up bass, while Billie handled lead guitar and vocals; drummer John seemed to be permanent. The still-in-high school lads found the coolest place in Berkeley to spend their weekends: 924 Gilman Street, a raggedy club made hip by virtue of how unhip it was. "A gathering of outcasts and freaks," Billie once tagged it. Gilman Street was a converted garage awash in graffiti, with dilapidated wood floorboards. All ages were welcome, and no alcohol was served. Almost anyone could play there, and almost everyone who did had the same raw punk sound.

Getting a record deal was the ultimate goal. To that end, Sweet Children recorded an EP called *1000 Hours* and shopped it around, lobbying hardest at Lawrence Livermore's Lookout! label, which was well-known in the Bay Area. The musician-cum-record label president eventually allowed the boys a shot at auditioning, but he didn't make it easy. He agreed to listen only if they made the two-hundred-mile drive up to Mendocino County.

The night of the tryout, everything that could go wrong did. The band arrived to find the place they were supposed to play shuttered down. Standing in the pouring rain, they did what came naturally—they broke in, only to discover there was no roof and no electricity. By then, already impressed with their tenacity (not to mention their audacity), Livermore went home, picked up a generator, and listened—along with twelve kids—as Green Day auditioned in the rain. "I was so impressed with the band and their attitude," remembers Lawrence, "playing just in front of a dozen people, that I hooked up with them immediately to record for Lookout. I never had any doubt about their potential musically. I thought they were great the first time I saw them."

With record contract firmly in hand, and a bunch of Billie-originals, they went into the recording studio. A few weeks later, after spending Lookout!'s allotted sum of five hundred dollars (a minuscule amount, but not an uncommon figure for a small, independent label), they emerged with their first official CD, *1,039/Smoothed Out Slappy Hours*. At that point, they rechristened themselves Green Day.

The music on *39/Smooth* is similar to Green Day's sound now, guitar-bashing punk with an unabashed pop beat. All the songs were short. Seventy percent of them related to girls, including "Disappearing Boy," "The One I Want," and "Why Do You Want Him?" One representative track, "At the Library," poignantly captured the pain and frustration of a boy too shy to approach a girl he pines for from afar. One critic called it "the best song ever written by a high schooler." For when *39/Smooth* came out,

Billie and Mike were still in high school, sixteen and seventeen years old.

What makes a Green Day composition? Billie says that songs come about when he "blows things out of proportion. When I dwell on something for a really long time, that happens. Say you hate somebody and you sit and think about every single possible way you could kill them. You're like, 'I fuckin' hate them.' That's what I like to write about. Blow it out of proportion and then come back to it later and think, 'that's kind of silly.' It's a good way to get it over fast."

Green Day hit the road to promote *39/Smooth*. That was the only way they could get the music out. Lookout! did not have the resources to send out many promotional copies; their distribution was uneven at best. There was no money for publicity or promotion, so word of mouth and power of foot would have to do. All dates were booked by the band members themselves. They crisscrossed the U.S.A. and went overseas as well. In spite of the financial obstacles, the grassroots tactics worked. Without the benefit even of college radio airplay, *39/Smooth* managed to sell 40,000 copies.

Roughing it took its toll, mostly on drummer John, who decided to pack it in when the band returned from Europe. About to go into the studio for album number two, Green Day had no drummer. Enter Tré, who'd developed into a stylish and flamboyant drummer. Billie and Mike knew him from Gilman Street, a place he, too, had hung out. And, of course, Tré was better known to Lawrence Livermore. Thus complete, the trio began work on their sophomore effort.

In 1992, *Kerplunk* was released, sounding, well . . . not very different from *39/Smooth*. Again, the songs had familiar themes: girls, the meaning of life, neurosis, insanity, alienation, coming-of-age. The madcap pace was the same, with the exception of two '70s-style ballads, "Christie Road," and "No One Knows." The big difference between the two was the method used to record *Kerplunk*. Although there was still no money to make it more polished than *39/Smooth*, there was an effort to make it sound like a live recording. Normally, each vocal track is recorded separately, then blended together for the final mix. For *Kerplunk*, Mike sang his backup vocals at the same time Billie did leads, which gave the record a live feel.

With the addition of Tré, Green Day's touring equipment got a boost. Tré's dad, Frank, a former bus driver who owned a small trucking company, converted an old bookmobile van and installed himself as chauffeur. Things were looking up. In support of *Kerplunk*, the boys embarked on three different tours. With each succeeding one, the cities hit (Chicago, L.A., New York) got bigger, and so did the crowds. Among the musically hip, word of mouth spread: Green Day was the "hottest new band on the indie scene." Record sales escalated, and *Kerplunk* broke all previous Lookout! sales records.

INTO THE BIGS: A WHOLE LOT OF DOOKIE

By 1993, Green Day was ready for the next step. Although they'd always be loyal to Lookout!, they needed the kind of support, and money, that only a major record label could supply. With the aid of professional managers Elliot Cahn and Jeff Saltzman, who circulated their demos around town, Green Day put themselves in play. They knew it was the right thing to do but nevertheless were plagued by doubts. Would they lose their cutting edge when they left the indie label? Would they have to compromise their fiercely independent streak? Would they be selling out?

Signing on with the right major label—Warner/Reprise—put those fears to rest. Their first endeavor for a major record company did little to change Green Day. Soon after the ink had dried on their new contract, Billie, Mike, and Tré went into the studio. Six weeks later, out came *Dookie*. It proved at least one thing: You can take the boys out of the indie scene, but you can't take the indie out of the boys.

From the record's title to its jacket—a humorous cartoon depicting (among other things) animals throwing their crap at people—it was completely irreverent. Best of all, the music itself hadn't changed. It was still every parent's nightmare and every teenager's dream. It was everything Green Day.

Dookie is heavy on crunchy pop guitar hooks, trebly bass, and brilliant vocal harmonies. The record sounds nearly as raw and unpredictable as the two that preceded it. This time, of course, it was done intentionally, not because there was no money to polish it. Yes, it's punk: There are no pretensions, no moralizing, no guitar heroics. And, yes, it's pop-hooky, melodic, and sometimes sing-along-able. "Pulling Teeth," in fact, sounds more like the early Beatles with its rough harmonies and simple hooks than anything ever done by the Sex Pistols. "A combination of the best pop hits and worst punk attitudes," is how one reviewer summed up *Dookie*. Pop core, punk-pop, neopunk, call it what you will. Green Day's been called it all.

Lyrically, it still depicts, according to one critic, "a pissed off state of mind." Odes to adolescent alienation, boredom, frustration, procrastination, and girls wind throughout. Billie is happy with the result. "I think I was more comfortable with my songwriting on this record than I ever was before," he admits. "I had a real good handle on what kind of melodies and hooks I wanted to come up with. Didn't rush myself, just let them come out naturally."

What came naturally were a bunch of tunes about things that "Mom and Dad will never understand," as they sing on "Coming Clean." The band may be in their twenties now and playing in a much bigger sandbox, but they still know what it feels like to be "seventeen and strung out on confusion," as they wail in "Burnout." Green Day can still plumb the teenage wasteland of procrastination ("no time for motivation; smoking my inspiration") as no other modern band can.

Then again, some songs are about nothing. "Longview," one of the defining songs on *Dookie*—about masturbation—was "cheap self-therapy for watching too much TV," Billie admits. "It was another case of writing about whatever mood I'm in."

Not all Green Day songs are Armstrong-autobiographical. "Basket Case," explains Billie, was mainly "about a friend who's pretty loopy, but a bit about myself as well—like seeing your own traits in other people where it's been taken to the total extreme. There are a lot more songs on this record that are about other people's experiences, even though I'm singing them in the first person."

Commercially, the biggest hit on *Dookie* was "When I Come Around," a song whose pop/hook sensibilities are stronger than any other track on the record: You actually can hum it. That one, "In the End," and "She" are Green Day's version of love songs. But they show growth. No longer simply about not getting the girl, these are about getting into a girl's head, trying to understand her, and creating relationships that work.

FAME, FORTUNE, and the FLIPSIDE
"Fame—it's everything I never dreamed of."   —Mike Dirnt

Although the music itself may have changed only imperceptibly, the number of fans exposed to Green Day after *Dookie* changed dramatically. With each new single released, accompanied by the requisite MTV video, fans seemed to multiply exponentially. They didn't just buy the CD—though an amazing number did: *Dookie* has sold over eight million copies and is still going strong—they packed the concert halls as well. Naturally, fans got their money's worth.

A Green Day concert is colorful: Billie often performs in a lavender clown suit; Mike hops around in a yellow jumpsuit. Tré has been known to show up in lipstick and a dress. Going him one better, Billie's bared all onstage. Reflecting the pure energy of the records, Green Day concerts are perpetual motion, irreverent, and loud. Billie, stroking the same guitar he had at eleven, yells obscenities into the crowd. Mike beats his head into the microphone, leaps around the stage, and into the mosh pit. They're never prepared with a song list—"We make it up as we go," Tré admits. Still, there is a method behind the madness. "It's all about making our audience feel like they're at home, communicating on an eye-level basis," Billie explains. Indeed, on a very primal level, Green Day *is* their audience. An unplanned mud-fight onstage at Woodstock '94 was something both Green Day and their audience got into.

But there is a downside to making it in the bigs. The band has felt the slings and arrows of the disenchanted: Original fans who believe, no matter what, that Green Day has sold out. The punk purists would not welcome them back, for instance, to 924 Gilman Street. More than any other band member, Mike has come under particular fire, amid accusations that while he rakes in the bucks, his family remains living below the poverty level. "I plan to deal with that," he has responded.

While Green Day is hardly immune to the ravings, they're also mature enough to know you can't please everyone. So they don't try. They choose to remain true to their roots their way. They steadfastly refuse any and all commercial endorsements—and have joined in a lawsuit with other groups against General Motors and *Rolling Stone* magazine for putting their photo in a car ad without their permission.

They haven't suddenly gone PC, either. They say what they feel, blasting back at their critics, even at the expense of their peers. "It's not how big you get, but how you get big," Tré philosophizes. "If you get big because you're shoved down everybody's throat, like Pearl Jam—I mean, MTV played the shit out of that band—then people won't appreciate you anymore."

What's important to them is loyalty: They have insisted that their original label, Lookout!, keep 100 percent of the royalties and rights to *39/Smooth* and *Kerplunk*. Because of *Dookie*, there's renewed interest in the band's early work, and that adds up to a lot of revenue for Lookout!. Green Day has also successfully kept their ticket prices down, playing arenas for what amounts to little more than the price of a movie ticket.

At the end of the day, according to

Billie, it's still all about what's between the grooves. "The most credibility you can have is to stay true to your music."

INSOMNIAC

Staying true to everything Green Day was exactly what they did on their eagerly anticipated *Dookie* follow-up. Titled *Insomniac* and released in October 1995, it was the kind of album you couldn't mistake for that of any other band. It featured fourteen songs—all performed in under thirty-three minutes of hyperactive spirit and spunk. But its fast and furious pace wasn't its only connection to Green Day's previous three albums—just like those, *Insomniac* was packed with punk-themed songs of despair, of hating your parents and hating yourself. Billie, once again the head composer, even tackled the question of whether a band that's no longer hungry or angry can stay true to its alt-punk roots. "Walking Contradiction" is not only the name of a song on *Insomniac*—it's Billie's answer.

Though most people felt Green Day hadn't strayed at all from their "bubble-punk" formula, there were a few who noted a new direction in *Insomniac*. Many of the songs are more belligerent and less melodic and accessible. You wouldn't, for instance, walk down the street humming "Geek Stink Breath" (the album's first, and very successful, single).

Perhaps the most astounding thing about *Insomniac*, when all was said and done, was its inability to sustain a lot of interest. Though the album debuted at a respectable number two on the charts, it didn't hold its position for long: After several weeks, it had fallen out of the Top Ten altogether.

Personally, the band is moving on. Tré's girlfriend, Lisea, gave birth to their first daughter, Ramona, last year. Billie, too, is a new father. He and his wife, Adrienne, became parents to Joey in March of 1995. It won't be surprising if Green Day's new material reflects what's going on in the band's personal lives—imagine what a Green Day lullaby would sound like!

What You Didn't Know about Green Day

◊ Billie, small and wired, is the quiet one, yet always the center of attention.

◊ Mike vacillates between serious & silly.

◊ Tré talks the most, offering commentary on every situation.

◊ Mike has a heart condition.

◊ Offstage, the trio is still always together, and describe themselves as "assholes trying to be nice guys."

◊ It's a Green Day all over the world: *Dookie* has sold over 1.4 million overseas.

◊ Where to Write: Green Day, c/o Warner/Reprise Records, 4000 Warner Boulevard, Burbank, CA 91522.

THE ANGST OF ALTERNATIVE

PLAYERS

JULIANA CDs

Only Everything (Atlantic/Mammoth) 1995

Become What You Are (Atlantic/Mammoth,
as The Juliana Hatfield three) 1993

Hey Babe (Mammoth) 1992

BLAKE BABIES CDs AND EPs (Juliana, plus John Strohm
on guitar and Freda Love Boner on bass)

Innocence and Experience (a Mammoth collection of takes) 1994

Rosy Jack (Mammoth) 1991

Sunburn (Mammoth) 1990

Earwig (Mammoth) 1989

Nicely, Nicely (Chewbud Records) 1987

JULIANA HATFIELD
singer, songwriter,
guitarist

Dean Fisher
bass

Josh Freese
drums

Mike Levesque
drums

49

Juliana
Hatfield

Juliana Hatfield

OPENING NOTES

Juliana Hatfield has been crowned alternative music's princess of teen angst. It's a crown the singer/songwriter bears uneasily. But then again, there's little she *is* comfortable with. Certainly not the descriptions of her music as "the chronicles of mope," or more flippantly, of herself as "this generation's Lesley Gore." While she appreciates her young fans, she wonders if their devotion roots her in permanent musical adolescence.

Juliana is publicly conflicted about lots of other things as well. She needs to be part of a band— but the minute she's part of one, she disbands it. She doesn't think she's a

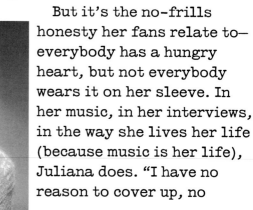

particularly accomplished guitarist, but gamely does the strumming on her album and onstage. She's frustrated by the limits of her voice, but bravely puts it out there. She claims that talking to the press makes her feel "dirty," yet when she has an album to plug, she does the deed and dishes the sound bites, even though they sometimes come back to haunt her—like the time she told *Spin* she was a virgin.

But it's the no-frills honesty her fans relate to— everybody has a hungry heart, but not everybody wears it on her sleeve. In her music, in her interviews, in the way she lives her life (because music is her life), Juliana does. "I have no reason to cover up, no concept of performing as an *act*. It's like life. I haven't come with an image. I just try to be honest about everything," is what she says in an interview. In a song, she puts it more artfully: "If life is a performance, and I am not an actor, am I supposed to lay down and die?" The alternative is to tell it like it is.

And honestly, there is no one on the alternative scene who delves more deeply, or accurately, into the recesses of adolescent agony. Take an album—*Hey, Babe*; *Become What You Are*; or *Only Everything*—pick a track, "Ugly," "My Sister," "What a Life," and press "start." Juliana "spins the bottle" and every time lands squarely on such "we've-all-been-there stuff" as feeling ugly, jealous, alone. Feeling like a voyeur in your own life, uncool, and, of course, feeling the "necessary" hurt of being in love, especially when it's the unrequited kind. Hers is not music to dance to, and you'd be hard-pressed to hum to very many tracks. But you sure can brood to it. And you sure can come away uplifted and inspired by it, too.

As she says, "a heart that hurts is a heart that works." Juliana Hatfield's beats loud and clear in the music she makes—touching a universal chord.

WHAT A LIFE

Juliana Hatfield believes in music as salvation. She knows it saved *her* life. In fact, it continues to do so. "Sometimes, I can't think of any other reason to be alive," she says matter-of-factly and

without the slightest trace of pathos.

The gut-wrenching honesty can seem like yet another contradiction. She may feel the pain of emotional barrenness as keenly as a pauper, but in reality, Juliana grew up comparatively privileged.

Her hometown is Duxbury, Massachusetts, a Boston burb she has disparagingly referred to in song as "Deluxe-bury." Nevertheless, it's only in song ("Feeling Massachusetts") that she's "gonna drown in this stinking town." Talk to her, and she doesn't cop to being that unhappy there. Out of place, maybe. Lonely, geeky, bored, definitely. But not so miserable. She was close to both parents, her fashion editor (for the *Boston Globe* newspaper) mom, as well as her dad, who (though divorced) clearly supported her musical leanings.

"I was born with the desire to make music," Juliana relates. "It's not like any band influenced me." By the age of five, she was making up little songs in her head; at six, she began piano lessons. It was Dad who gave her that first guitar when she was ten. "I actually only picked it up just because it was there," Juliana tells. In fact, she only toyed briefly with the instrument that would become so important later on, then put it away until college.

The teenage Juliana was a "bit of a loner, but willfully so." In high school, she could've been welcomed into any one of numerous cliques, but chose to stay just outside the mainstream. "I was breaking away, trying to find out who I was," she explains. "I thought the best way was to be on my own. In high school, there's a lot of peer pressure. You can be easily influenced. I didn't want to fall prey to that."

Not that she was a pariah or anything. There were friends with whom she "did stuff"—sneak out of the house, stay out late, go to parties. But she did sports with other friends: Juliana was a team player in high school tennis, gymnastics, field hockey, and soccer. She also worked on her school's literary magazine.

There was little need to rebel against her parents, because they were basically cool with whatever she did. "They knew that I had the sense not to fuck up. And I didn't, at least not in the typical ways. I didn't do drugs or anything self-destructive. My willful isolation was my only form of rebellion."

The rock band that attracted Juliana most in those days was the Replacements. It wasn't just the music she related to, more the band's attitude—or

lack of one. "They were just four guys who played rock. They didn't have that stuck-up rock star attitude. Instead, they were self-deprecating. They weren't afraid to fuck up, they showed their humanness. They were raw, but melodic."

Just about the time she got into the Replacements, Juliana experienced her

own personal epiphany. It suddenly dawned on her that there was never any real choice. Music was something she had to do. At the risk of sounding otherworldly, she explains: "I had a mystical experience, and stuff like that doesn't happen to me much. I was in my house in the late afternoon and there was a lot of sun coming in. I looked over at the corner and sort of saw myself singing. And it was the future. And I knew that was what I had to do."

But she didn't pass go and head directly for music school. There was a stint, albeit short, at Boston University first. But practically as soon as she got there, she realized she was in the wrong place at a critical time. "I really needed to go to music school," she understood just then. Serendipitously, the renowned Berklee School of Music was nearby. All those years of piano lessons allowed her to bypass the audition process, but as soon as she enrolled, she switched her concentration to vocals. And began concentrating on her first group.

(BLAKE) BABY STEPS

The band that would become Juliana's first started as a duo. The Blake Babies was the creation of fellow Berklee buds John Strohm and Freda Love Boner. They saw in Juliana a kindred spirit. "We thought we were the only weird ones here, but Juliana . . . would just stare at the floor in her leather jacket and floppy ponytail," they've said. They asked her to become their bass player and front person.

It was Juliana's musical christening, a period she describes rapturously. "When I first wanted to write music and play with other people, it was an amazing spiritual thing. An awakening. It was just so important to me. 'Cause up until I found a band and started writing, I really felt alone. I wanted to play music but I didn't know how to get a band together. When I finally did, it was such a big thing in my life. It was more important than anything to me."

During those heady (at times, shaved heady), halcyon days, the Blake Babies rehearsed continually, performed anywhere and everywhere, and constantly experimented with their sound and their look. At one particularly memorable gig—Juliana's since dubbed it the worst ever—at a college in South Carolina, the band was trashed by "a room full of drunk jocks, who [yelled sexual epithets] at us for our shaved heads. But we got the last laugh—we poured beer on their jock heads."

Doing music that was beautiful yet barbed, which combined tuneful guitar strumming with hard-edged confrontational lyrics, the Blake Babies soon carved their niche in Boston's burgeoning alternative music scene. In the mid-'80s, other musicians there of like influence included Bullet LaVolta, Moving Targets, and the Lemonheads' Evan Dando, with whom Juliana would eventually be press-linked.

Getting a record contract was the plan.

It wasn't easy to implement. "We sent demos to independent labels, but no one wanted to sign us," Juliana recounts. So the Blake Babies used the back door. "We went into a record pressing plant—you give them the tapes and the artwork, and they press you an actual record. We paid for 1,000 copies, put it on our own label that we called Chewbud Records, and shopped it ourselves to college radio stations. Some of them actually played it."

One label who liked what they heard was Chapel Hill, North Carolina–based Mammoth Records. In 1987, they signed the Blake Babies and released the band's first CD, *Nicely, Nicely*. Which pretty much describes the band's musical progression through their next three albums. The harmony was just on the outside, though; the inner workings of the band weren't—working, that is. And Juliana would be the one to end it. "The Blake Babies were three distinct musical entities contributing equally, making decisions—and fighting against each other," she's explained of their 1991 breakup.

The dissolution of the Blake Babies marked the beginning of Juliana's "I need a band/I can't deal with having a band" struggle. She had her own personal musical vision, but often felt she couldn't do it alone. The insecurity and vulnerability were just too overwhelming. She'd remain conflicted about the band thing for years to come. "Breaking up [the Blake Babies] was the right thing to do, 'cause you gotta move on," she said bravely at the time. She was "sick of

democracy." But on the other hand, being out on her own, without the protective layer of other players, terrified her. "I got scared for a while. Stupid thoughts like, 'If this goes on much longer, I'll have to kill myself.' It sounds really melodramatic, all those thoughts you have when you're really depressed, like, 'I'm gonna be alone forever, I'm gonna die alone, I'm never gonna find another band so I might as well kill myself.'"

Instead—like the artist she truly is—she poured all those feelings into her music and her first solo effort, 1992's *Hey Babe*. Critically praised, commercially ignored, *Hey Babe* appeared blatantly autobiographical: teeming with songs about being in love with someone who doesn't love you ("Everybody Loves Me But You," and "I See You"), eating disorders, and self-mutilation. Perhaps the defining song on *Hey Babe* was "Ugly," about how it feels when you think you're less than zero, 'Ugly—with a capital U.' To its fans, *Hey Babe* was "a pinnacle of low-self-esteem record." There it was: Expressing what it feels like to be the geek was classic Juliana—no one put those heart-wrenching feelings to music with more gut-wrenching sincerity.

Her unblinking honesty in the grooves is only matched by her honesty about the record. She didn't revere it nearly as much as her fans did. "I didn't really like *Hey Babe*, but I learned from it. I learned what I didn't want to do on the next one."

THE JULIANA HATFIELD THREE— BECOMING WHAT SHE IS

"That's what life is about, just becoming who you are and you want to be . . ." —Juliana Hatfield

In 1993, recruiting old schoolmate Dean Fisher on bass ("He used to have a crush on me in high school," Juliana dishes) and Todd Phillips (of Bullet LaVolta) on drums, Juliana sought to create a quasi-democratic musical union, reserving the spotlight and the most power for herself. To make that clear, she called her combo the Juliana Hatfield three. The lowercase punctuation wasn't a typo: It was a signal. She figured, "I like the security of a band, they make me able to play heavier, but with this band, things are slightly more in my favor. I have more control and more of the attention is on me." With that in place—or at least she thought—work began in earnest on the next album.

Stung by the criticism that the songs on *Hey Babe* were too "head-slappingly obvious," Juliana set out to make her second album somewhat more obtuse—but never any less honest. Elusive, ambiguous lyrics set against visceral, almost giddy, guitar work, the songs on that sophomore effort, *Become What You Are,* touch places she herself may never have been—except, of course, in her heart.

"My Sister," which has taken on a life of its own as Juliana's signature song, is the prime example. "I hate my sister, she's such a bitch. . . . I love my sister, she's

the best. . . . I miss my sister, why'd she go?" Juliana wailed plaintively—and anyone who's ever had those potent mixed feelings about a sister exclaimed, *"Exactly!"* That tune captured the hate-love ambiguity so perfectly that music journalists and fans were astounded to find out that Juliana didn't *have* a sister. "It's just a song about feelings, images," she insists. "I've experienced those feelings, but not with a blood sister. You can have those feelings with friends, brothers, parents."

On *Become What You Are* Juliana began writing more about feelings than tangible events in her life. "I am inspired by books, movies, nature, people I know and also strangers," she explains. Don't ask Juliana what her songs *mean,* though—for the most part, she'd rather they be about whatever the listener finds in them. "It's futile to try and figure it out because I contradict myself all the time," Juliana says. "The songs don't capture me—maybe little pieces of me mixed up with the things I make up that are better or worse than me. I've been accused of being too sincere in the past with *Hey Babe*—you do get ridiculed and I was probably affected by that. My lyrics are a little more cryptic now, but that's how I like it. It's more interesting. I never meant to be so open."

Still, "Supermodel" seemed, at first listen, obvious. What else could a song that goes, "The highest paid piece of ass, you know it's not gonna last," be if not an ode to the superficiality and fleeting fame of faceless mannequins deified by the media? Well, how about Juliana's own feelings of being perceived as a "thing"—in her case, just another chick-guitar-player—rather than an individual? Juliana acknowledges, "People try to pigeonhole me, but I don't fit into the usual categories. Maybe I'll transcend the whole gender thing, but I'll still be interesting because there aren't as many women doing it."

Juliana's love songs are (for want of a better word) ambivalent. "I can never relate to those 'I love you, baby' songs," she explains. "My experience with love is more like Dinosaur Jr.'s 'In a Jar.' It's from the point of view of a bug. That's how love makes you feel, like a little insect. Small, inconsequential, ineffectual, and at the mercy of someone else." An interesting take on a complicated and personal subject—and her songs reflect that twist.

Become What You Are propelled Juliana to alterna-poster-girl status, something she was unprepared for. Suddenly being heralded as the voice of a genre baffled her. "I didn't feel like I deserved the attention I was getting," she said as her photo was plastered on the cover of music as well as fashion magazines. "I was just sort of going along for the ride, feeling,

'Why is this happening?' Because the record and the amount it sold didn't really warrant all that."

Once again, Juliana's insecurities were showing. "I'm still frustrated by the limitations of my voice," she said in one interview after the next. "Every time I sing, I'm struggling to overcome my limitations." Indeed, she *is* an alternative to such trained voices as Mariah Carey or Whitney Houston. Juliana's is a reedy, thin vocal instrument, but maybe not so unlike that of her fans who sing along to her records. Her guitar playing was far from where she wanted it to be as well. Later on, she'd admit to being afraid of the instrument. In spite of the album title, it seemed she had a long way to go before becoming comfortable with who she was.

The band thing came up again, and once again Juliana let the world in on her conflicted emotions. "I wanted a band, but I didn't really want to commit to it. I didn't want to throw myself into being part of a band wholeheartedly. That's why I put my name on it, but I also called it a band." So when her drummer departed, Juliana felt more liberated than bummed. "They were just a backup group, anyway. I decided to go ahead as a soloist."

ONLY EVERYTHING

"If I was simply a craftsman, I would have done a record like this a long time ago. But I'm not good at faking stuff..."
—Juliana Hatfield

It took two years for Juliana to produce another record—her longest span between releases so far. Yet the growth displayed on *Only Everything* might have taken another artist even longer. In 1995 Juliana Hatfield grew into her own songwriting/vocal/guitaring skin. And it shows. She's as honest as ever, and ever more obtuse lyrically. And not so incidentally, *instrumentally,* we're not in acoustic—balladry land anymore.

As *Time* magazine put it, "One of the hardest things to write is a song that has no specific meaning, but nonetheless conjures up powerful feelings or ideas, a song that rings true emotionally." Juliana just gets better and better at that. "My songs are less specific and more open to interpretation now. I can write about anything and it can have whatever meaning people give it. While giving people more to sink their teeth into, it also gives me more opportunity to see art in more places. I used to write about what was going on in my head—now I can write a song about a piece of dirt, or whatever."

Well, maybe not a piece of dirt, but certainly about a last-ditch warning to a heroin addict friend, as on "Dying Proof." Which, because it came out around the time of Kurt Cobain's death, was widely interpreted to be about Nirvana's doomed leader. Yet Juliana protests, "I wrote that before he died, and I was not thinking of Kurt—but I can see how people might think it's about him. I was actually thinking of what it would feel like to save someone's life, to jump in front of a bullet aimed at someone else."

The ragged rocker, "Dumb Fun," which includes the head-scratching line, "Had a heart by accident," was composed by stringing together random passages from a notebook of ideas she'd been keeping; "OK, OK" is her rendition of an imagined fight between a fictional couple. If the racing rocker "What a Life" was inspired by a photo, as she tells, it begs the question of what exactly she was looking at when she composed it. Icky, sticky images of looking at a life (her own?) that's by turns "grungy! dirty! smelly! fetid! sweaty! hopeless! wretched!" all barked at a pace that's pounding! is unsettling to say the least. (The second single off *Only Everything,* it bombed commercially.)

The catchy, hooky, "Universal Heartbeat," the album's first single, asserts that it's better to feel pain than deny feelings altogether. "A heart that hurts is a heart that works" goes the chorus. Which may be small consolation to the hurting, but inspiring nevertheless. "It's better to feel something than nothing," insists the artist who obviously knows. "Even if you're in pain, psychic pain, it shows that you still have a heart. At least you're not totally cold and numb and turned off."

Perhaps the biggest change from *Become* to *Only* was in the riffs: It *rocks*. Of "What a Life," arguably the hardest rocker on *Only Everything*, Juliana laughs, "It's not Black Sabbath, but it's still pretty heavy." Partly, the tougher tone happened because Juliana willed this record to be different. But these days, she's also a more relaxed musician. "When I relaxed, I started to rock more. I'm much more comfortable with my guitar. I used to be afraid of it; not anymore. I realize now I'm the master of my guitar. I have to make it work for me. That's what it's there for. It wants to be told what to do." Added to the grubby rock guitar riffs are r 'n' b electric piano tickles—Juliana played keys on several tunes—which makes for a supercharged CD.

Only Everything marked a big change for Juliana and was greeted with strong, and strongly mixed, emotions. While some hailed her moving beyond the sweetly acoustic to the more assertive, others slammed her attempt to juxtapose her

high, delicate, "girlish voice" with the low, slashing guitars. "Her voice doesn't keep pace with the roaring guitars," groused one review. "It's the girliest grunge record in history."

Juliana herself is happy with *Only Everything*. "I felt relaxed and comfortable like never before. This record felt like a gift, everything fell into place. It seemed like the record was just handed to me as a payoff for all the creative frustration I've had. After eight years of waiting, it finally happened. Here is what you wanted to achieve. Oh, finally."

TOUCHING YOU, TOUCHING ME

Does this mean that she has finally, then, become what she is? In one way, she says, "No. I haven't gotten to where I'm making the music I want to. I'm on the path, but I haven't gotten to the ultimate yet."

But in another way, most definitely. For the getting there is what it's all about for Juliana—that, and the people she reaches along the way. What Juliana hears all the time from her fans is variations on one theme: "Your music got me through the rough times. I don't know what I would have done without your records." And at the end of the day, that really is what it all comes down to.

"The fact that my music touches people makes me feel really good, like I'm doing something worthwhile in this life, touching someone like that. It's a lot better than anything, more satisfying than selling a million records. Commercial success doesn't mean anything." While the other stuff means . . . only everything.

What You Always Wanted to Know About Juliana

BIRTHDAY: July 27, 1968.

EVAN DANDO . . . "and I are friends. We'll always be friends. He's my friend. I'm his friend. Evan and I always liked each other, but we both knew that as a couple it wouldn't work. We're both so . . . crazy and egotistical."

SONG AUDIENCES LOVE MOST: "My Sister" and "Spin the Bottle."

SONG JULIANA WISHES AUDIENCES WOULD LOVE MORE: "Congratulations." "I thought it would make the crowds really crazy . . . it rocks . . . it bugs me out [that fans don't react more strongly to it] because it's so fun to play."

HER BROMIDE FOR LONELINESS ON THE ROAD: "Sleep."

WHAT SHE DID FOR THE FIRST TIME IN 1995 THAT SHE'D NEVER DONE BEFORE (BUT YOU PROBABLY THOUGHT SHE DID): Dived into the crowd. "I liked it a lot."

PEOPLE ALWAYS THINK I . . . "am serious—when I'm not!"

WHERE SHE WRITES: Alone in her apartment.

WHEN SHE WRITES: Late at night.

ABOUT THAT ACTING GIG: Juliana played a homeless angel on a classic episode of TV's *My So-Called Life* (she also wrote a song for the sound track, "Make It Home"). But she isn't about to put down her guitar. "I'm not an accomplished actress, I didn't have enough technique to really know what I was doing. I don't have any other acting jobs coming up."

LIVES NOW: Juliana split Boston for New York City.

SHE LOVES HER FANS: Juliana never cancels concerts—she's even played in ice storms—and communicates most often with them on computer. TIP: If you communicate with her on-line, please spell her name correctly (one *L*, one *N*)—she's got kind of a thing about that.

IF SHE WASN'T MAKING MUSIC: "I'd be a rotting vegetable."

FAVE RECORD OF ALL TIME: Dinosaur Jr.'s "You're Living All over Me."

WHERE TO WRITE: In fact, Juliana asks that her address not be printed.

THE PISSED-OFF SOUND
OF ALTERNATIVE

CDs

Ask for It (Geffen) 1995

Live Through This (Geffen) 1994

Pretty on the Inside (Caroline Records) 1991

EP

Retard Girl (Sympathy for the Record Industry) 1990

SINGLES

"Beautiful Son" (City Slang) 1993

"Dicknail" (Subpop) 1991

"Teenage Whore" (City Slang) 1991

PLAYERS

Courtney Love
singer, songwriter, guitar

Eric Erlandson
guitar

Patty Schemel
drums

Melissa auf der Maur
bass

Past Players **Kristen Pfaff** (DECEASED, 1994) bass **Caroline Rue** drums **Jill Emery** bass

65

AWARDS & REWARDS

Live Through This, which has sold over one million copies, was named Best Album of the Year, in 1994 by both *Rolling Stone* and *Spin* magazines. It also won the *Village Voice* newspaper's critics poll.

hole

HOW THEY GOT THEIR NAME

"It's from a conversation with my mom," Courtney once confessed. "I told her what a terrible childhood I'd had and she said, 'Well, Courtney, you can't walk around with a big hole inside yourself because of it.' And I thought, different kinds of anger and stuff came from my hole—this hole that needs to be fed. That angst inside a person is like their hole, like when you feel that emptiness and you have to feed it. Besides, we're the kind of band that sucks you in."

PEERING INTO THE KEYHOLE

Holey, moley, Courtney Love is pissed. The explosive grunge diva who dug this Hole has become best known for her ferocious temper and atrocious behavior. Rarely a week goes by when there's not some Courtney controversy in the news. One week, she's punching out a female rocker; another, she's punching out a fan. One night, she's chasing one of her late husband's ex's down the street; another, she's screaming expletives at her audience, pitching fits *and* guitars in their faces. Alone, she could keep an entire law firm in business.

Courtney says—make that, screams—what's on her mind, consequences be damned. She's outrageous, outspoken, in and out of rehab. Rumors of drug abuse dog her; as do those that allege authorities might take her daughter away. She dresses like a (her word) "kinderwhore"; smears lipstick across her mouth, mats rather than combs her defiantly messy hair.

All that and, of course, her once and forever connection to late husband Kurt Cobain and Nirvana *always* overshadow Hole's music. And that's a shame.

As veteran rock journalist Lisa Robinson put it, "None of [Courtney's contentious behavior] would matter if she hadn't made a great record, which she did."

Pissed off, punky, loud, and angry, Courtney's really no different on record than she is off. But guitar in hand, all that raunch and rage mutates into songs that are brilliant, compelling, twisted, raw, and achingly vulnerable. From the seething antirape "Was she asking for it? Was she asking nice?" to the shockingly violent "Pieces of Jennifer's Body" to the hopeful innocence of "I tell you everything/I hope that you won't tell on me," Hole songs are alternatively soothing and seething; furious and poignant.

Modern rock's bad girl has always been—ironically—more like Eddie Vedder than any of her alt sisters: Juliana might "hate" her sister; Courtney'd just as soon rip her to shreds. Dolores declares a love affair over when there's "no need to argue"; Courtney can't help firing that last shot, "Fuck *you!*"

Audiences have long held a hate/Love relationship with Hole. For Courtney is the bad girl, the one at school who's been caught smoking in the girls' room and experimenting with other unmentionables. But she's also the girl a part of us would secretly like to be. But most of us don't dare go out on that dangerous emotional limb—so we *Live Through This*, Hole's music.

MISS WORLD
"Someday you will ache like I ache."
—"Doll Parts"

Courtney's life story reads like so much pulp fiction; she swears it's all true. It certainly goes a long way toward explaining her seething rage and revenge songs. It also goes a long way toward explaining (though not excusing) her outrageous offstage behavior.

All her life, Courtney Love has yearned to be "the girl with the most cake." Instead, she's always ended up the girl with the emptiest plate. Constantly rejected and ejected, she felt unwanted, ugly, and betrayed for the first half of her life. She's been lashing out, trying to get revenge ever since.

Growing up, it seemed no one wanted her. Tossed around like a discarded doll, Courtney was shipped among a succession of caretakers and dragged all over the map. She was in and out of schools—many were reform schools. She didn't even have the same name throughout her childhood.

Her birth certificate reads Love Michelle Harrison. She was born in San Francisco on July 9, 1965. Her father, Hank Harrison, a Grateful Dead fanatic-turned-small book publisher, and mother, Linda Carroll, an heiress to an eyeglass fortune-turned-therapist, divorced before their only child's first birthday. Both parents fought to keep her. As it turned out, neither really wanted her.

At the age of three, she was renamed Courtney Michelle Harrison. But with Linda's subsequent remarriages, the little girl would be Courtney Rodriquez and Courtney Manely. She'd move from San Francisco, California, to Eugene, Oregon, and later, when Linda Carroll came into her inheritance and became a therapist, to a mansion in Marcola, Oregon.

A few years later, Linda and husband number three split for New Zealand to start a sheep farm. They did not take third grader Courtney with them. To this day, the rocker is not exactly sure why. "I guess I was too much trouble," she shrugs. Trouble is what has followed ever since. Courtney bounced between caretakers (family friends, as opposed to family, for the most part), therapists and schools—which she often got kicked out of for misconduct—and began to shoplift. She was not popular. "Kids hated me," she admitted.

So did her caretakers, as it turned out. Courtney was shipped to New Zealand, but once there, was not embraced by relatives. Instead, Courtney was sent to live with another family friend and began what she remembers as a happy time in her life. "I had friends at school and thought I was doing really well," was the tale she told in *Spin* magazine. "I thought this family friend really liked me." Wrong again.

Ejected from New Zealand, she then bounced between Eugene and Portland, Oregon, where she lived with the family of a previous stepdad. Back at school in the States, the downward spiral began in earnest. "I'd been livin' in New Zealand," Courtney said. "I was really into the [Bay City] Rollers, I had a David Bowie hairdo. I was a freak at my school." She further claims to have been "a very quiet/bordering on autistic child," yet did not sit still for the schoolroom abuse. "I got the shit beat out of me enough times so I started to become really scrappy. I was a runt, no tits, no period, no puberty—I was the last girl on the planet with tits; I was the last girl that would ever hit puberty—so I got picked on. And I realized that I can fight really well if I just pretend I'm going to murder the person."

Although she was in too much pain to know it at the time, that hurtful period would one day be translated into song. "Retard Girl" is one of Hole's very first singles. "It's about what it's like to be picked on at school," Courtney would later explain. "It's about me."

Juvenile Courtney soon became juvenile delinquent Courtney. She purposely tried to get into trouble shoplifting at the mall. She once lifted a KISS T-shirt; her mother turned her in. She shuttled between reform schools for her efforts. At least one positive thing happened in one detention center, however: An intern turned her on to the kind of music that turned *her* on. "I started listening to the Pretenders, Squeeze, and the Sex Pistols," she recounted. "I decided then that I was going to be a rock star."

Because Mom was an heiress, one thing Courtney could count on was a trust fund. In her early teens, she took it and went about making that dream a reality. It was—to say the least—a circuitous route. Round, like a hole.

THE (W)HOLE TRUTH

"Hole doesn't work unless it's scary, unless it's intensely vulnerable. It's as real as I can get."
—Courtney Love

The Courtney saga has been well documented; not so Hole's history. Contrary to popular assumption, the band does have one. It predates *Live Through This*; it predates *Pretty on the Inside*—it certainly predates Kurt Cobain.

With her trust fund money, Courtney moved to Portland and immediately found the underground music scene. Hooking up with new friends Ursula Wehr and Robin Barbur, she formed her first band, the punky Sugar Baby Doll. It wasn't a steady gig. Over the next decade, Courtney would globe-hop, zigzagging from Portland to Taiwan, San Francisco to Japan, Seattle to Spain, Minneapolis and New York to Ireland and

England. She alternately attended college (Portland State, San Francisco State, San Francisco Art Institute, and Dublin's Trinity College), worked as a stripper, and hung out with bands. Tagged a groupie, she nevertheless soaked up vital musical lessons.

At sixteen, Courtney joined an early incarnation of the pioneering punk/metal band Faith No More. She hung out for a year before quitting. "They refused to look at my lyrics," the novice songwriter explained. A big issue, as Courtney was beginning to strongly believe, "In a song I think you should have something to say."

Sugar Baby Doll re-formed—this time with singer Kat Bjelland (now famous for Babes in Toyland)—broke up, came together again. The third time, Kat came with L7's Jennifer Finch. "The need was always there to play as hard as any guy." And these girls played it hard. They weren't particularly good, however. Courtney confesses, "We were really cheesy." She hopes those tapes never come out. After dissolving Sugar Baby Doll, Courtney played briefly with Kat and Lori Barbiero in Babes in Toyland. During this time, Courtney was struggling to learn guitar. It was an uphill battle, as she can now freely admit: "[Musician] Joe Strummer once told me, 'Courtney, you are the worst guitarist I have ever heard.'"

Undaunted, in 1989, she relocated to Los Angeles, determined to start from scratch. The ad she placed in LA's alternate music press, *Recycler*, was for a guitar player. It was answered by Eric Erlandson. Courtney liked him right away. "He was a tall, skinny blond and he knew who Sonic Youth were." He was hired. And so, the core of Hole had been dug: Drummer Caroline Rue and bass player Jill Emery rounded out the band in its earliest days.

The punk-rocking quartet signed almost immediately with an indie label out of Santa Monica called Sympathy for the Record Company. "It's the coolest record label in America," Courtney enthused at the time. "The guy that runs it is totally sincere and totally honest." The band went to work.

Hole songs then, as they are now, were Courtney compositions—and her natural-born rage has always found its way into them. That, more than anything, is what has defined the band. Courtney may have been abandoned, bruised, and abused, but she has always come back fighting in her music. "I may lie a lot," she once confessed, "but never in my lyrics."

The group's very first release was a three-track 45 titled *Retard Girl*. It contained that song—a female version of Pearl Jam's "Jeremy"—and another called "Phone Bill Song." The latter was made memorable not only by its ranting, top-of-the-lungs delivery, but by lyrics such as, "She's a bimbo playing on the damn phone."

Just as Courtney could never be pinned down and pigeonholed, neither could the band: Despite enthusiasm for

Sympathy for the Record Company, Hole bore through indie labels much as their leader had hopscotched through life. The single "Dicknail" came out on Seattle's Subpop label—a flip through the lyrics reveals it to be a primitive version of "Asking for It,"—and another, "Teenage Whore," was first released on the City Slang label.

Hole's earliest press clips, in fact, allude to an interesting musical—and personal—alliance. Hole's first songs were produced by a musician named Falling James, then lead singer for the group Falling Trains. He is further identified as Courtney's husband. There is also some allusion to Courtney releasing a solo record on the "K" label as well, doing minimalist garage pop.

PRETTY ON THE INSIDE

"There's a part of me that wants to have a grindcore band and another that wants to have a Raspberries-type pop band." —Courtney Love

In 1991, Hole signed with yet another label, Caroline Records, an indie subsidiary of Virgin, and put out its first full-length album, *Pretty on the Inside*. Courtney felt it presented "chick-rock" at its hardest and most honest. At the time, she explained, "There's been so

much white male posturing in rock, that what's important to me is getting across the female perspective—and that includes both rage and vulnerability."

Courtney further hoped her record would prove inspirational. "I want every girl in the world to pick up a guitar and start screaming," she declared. (Interestingly, today her attitude has done a 180. "I want to slap any girl who comes up to me and says how I've inspired her," she recently said.)

Pretty on the Inside was Courtney inside and out. "These songs are about my own weaknesses and impurities; things about myself that I hate, paranoias, petty concerns and pithy, pathetic things that are inside of me," she described. They included "Teenage Whore," inspired by one of the many times Courtney got kicked out of the house, and "Good Sister/Bad Sister," in which Eric's howling guitars combined with Courtney's churlish vocals for maximum effect.

Pretty on the Inside received mixed reviews. Loud and noisy, at least one reviewer dubbed it "headache-inducing." Another put it more diplomatically, writing, "it challenges mainstream audiences

with its raw power." Thumbs-up types saw it as "a chilling rock vision that fixates on the power of noise."

Courtney herself is less complimentary about *Pretty on the Inside* these days. In a recent MTV profile, she admitted, "I was consciously self-conscious. I was intimidated by Sonic Youth and Pussy Galore. That was lame."

Hole might have continued plugging away, and perhaps begun work on their next album, had Courtney not gotten involved right then with a certain charismatic leader of a very hot band.

The band was Nirvana, and when Kurt Cobain entered her life, everything changed. Hole's history was forever altered; some would say tainted. That the pair fell in love, married, had a child, and endured a turbulent, often drug-fueled, violent relationship has been written about ad nauseam. There's less out there about Kurt's influence on Hole, however. Yet he contributed to drummer Patty Schemel's joining the band to replace Caroline. Soon after, Jill Emery was also gone. Eric Erlandson recruited Minneapolis native Kristen Pfaff. "That's when we really took off," Courtney has said. "All of a sudden we became a real band."

The real band inked with yet another record company—this one, Geffen, the same to which Nirvana was already signed.

LIVE THROUGH THIS
"Rock is all about writing your own script—
it's all about pioneering."   —Courtney Love

When *Live Through This* was recorded—but not yet released—the prediction by those who'd heard it was that Courtney would become more famous than Kurt, that her album would eclipse Nirvana's, that she would prove herself to be equally if not more talented than her icon husband. What's more, Kurt agreed: "She's so Goddamned good," he opined passionately. If there was artistic competition between the two, it surfaced only rarely. For one thing, Courtney believed in the power of absorbing rock 'n' roll vibes. "Even if I were talentless, after seeing Nirvana 10 million times, how could I not write an okay new-wave record?" For another, she freely admitted that envy fueled

creativity. One night she spent listening to the beginnings of Nirvana's *Nevermind*, "I was so jealous of those songs, that I had to try to top them . . . they were so fiercely great." That was the night she wrote "Violet," the track that opens *Live Through This*.

Live Through This should have been a career-making album. An early review called it "brilliant, the most compelling record of the year." The dozen songs were by turns harsh and daring, raw and cathartic, with compact melodies and harrowing lyrics. It was made all the more poignant by Courtney's delivery—her throaty, ragged voice ricocheted from naked vulnerability to psychotic rage. That said, Hole's second album was more pop-influenced and commercial than *Pretty on the Inside*. But that doesn't

mean Courtney had calmed down: There's nothing middle-of-the-road about *Live Through This*—it's as hard hitting and angry as alternative gets.

Being used, and then discarded, feeling cheap, betrayed, taking revenge and taking responsibility ("I made my bed I'll lie in it; I made my bed I'll cry in it" is the chorus of "Miss World") are the themes that wind through *Live Through This*. No politics, no social commentary— it's all about how badly men treat women. Or, put another way, the relationships described on disc do little to fill the "hole" of need.

On "Violet" Courtney seethes, "when they get what they want, they never want it again," and then defiantly yells, "go on, take everything" [not only my body but my self-respect and my soul],

"take everything/I *want* you to! Go on take everything/take everything I *dare* you to!" But in the second verse, it's she who has become the hardened user: "When I get what I want/I never want it again. . . ."

The violence of rape and murder is chillingly described in "Jennifer's Body," from the soothing/shocking betrayal of "just relax, just relax, just go to sleep," to the "pieces of Jennifer's body" later found.

"Asking for It" is about degradation ("every time I sell myself to you/I feel a little bit cheaper than I need to") and date rape. Courtney viciously attacks the Neanderthal "blame the victim" mentality when she spits out the rhetorical lines, "Was she asking for it? Was she asking nice? Was she asking for

it? Did she ask you twice?"

The best-known and arguably best song on the album, however, is the aching, heartbreaking "Doll Parts." What's it like to be married to the hottest rock star on the planet? According to this track, it doesn't make you feel whole—"I am/doll parts/doll eyes/doll hearts." It makes you yearn to be so special, "the girl with the most cake." But having to share that rock God with the world is tough—"Yeah, they really want you/they really want you/ they really do," she acknowledges of the fans. "Yeah, they really want you . . . but I do too," she quietly begs. No one can understand the ache and the hurt. The best-known, most repeated line from "Doll Parts" is the most poignant, especially as the whisper slowly builds to a scream with each repetition: "Someday, you will ache like I ache."

Those words turned out to be ominously prescient, as Live Through This will be tainted forever by a case of the worst timing of any record ever to come out. It debuted a week before the gun shot heard round the music world. When Kurt Cobain killed himself, Courtney's life would never be the same—Hole's music would never be listened to the same way again. Suddenly, the title of the album took on a ghoulish tone as did such well-known lyrics as (from "Miss World") "Somebody kill me/give me pills," and of course, "If you live through this with me, I swear I will die for you" (from "Asking for It").

For a while it seemed the gaping wound of Kurt's suicide would only get wider:

The subsequent drug-related death of bass player Kristen Pfaff dealt another blow to Courtney and the band. It seemed to close the lid on Live Through This.

AND THE BAND PLAYED ON
"Courtney Love is irrepressible."
—Billy Corgan of Smashing Pumpkins

Courtney Love is nothing if not a survivor. With the aid of ever-faithful and sturdily loving Eric Erlandson—"the glue that keeps me together," Courtney confessed—the band slowly regrouped. Melissa Auf der Maur, recruited by Eric, took over on bass and backup vocals. Getting back to performing was tough, but cathartic. "Her job is a singer in a rock band and she's good at her job—it's her saving grace," offered ex-manager Danny Goldberg. "Like others struggling with bereavement, she went back to work."

It was anything but a smooth re-entry into the music zone. In the months after Kurt's suicide and Kristen's death, the spotlight was never off Courtney. And she's never been one not to give 'em something to talk about. And so the Courtney antics once again threatened to take over: The punk princess harassed a flight attendant; got thrown off America Online; overdosed on a prescription drug and had to be rushed to the hospital.

The MTV Unplugged concert, as well as The Hole Story interview—and, to a lesser extent, 1995's Lollapalooza, which Hole headlined—might have put the focus back on the music. (Admittedly, the crazed moshing and backstage shenanigans once again threatened to obscure everything.) The MTV interview, however, revealed a quieter, saner Courtney—one who told her own story and renounced drugs. "It's really, really, really wrong to romanticize [drugs]," she opined. "And part of romanticizing it is talking about it. Everyone who takes drugs thinks 'I'm the one who can beat [addiction]'— yeah, six million junkies *are* wrong," she added sarcastically. She also gave her band the credit it deserves, and expressed a wish to get back to performing, because, "When we play, the Courtney thing goes away."

They played— stirringly, powerfully, beautifully—on *Unplugged*. Gone was the shock-shtick; in its place was just the music. Hole performed songs from *Live Through This* and did their version of Duran Duran's "Hungry Like the Wolf," as well as the unreleased Kurt composition "You Got No Right," which bears the ironic verse, "Things have never been so swell/I have never been so well."

It was the first time in a long time that the music took center stage. Perched on a stool, legs akimbo, guitar slung low, Courtney looked every inch the rock star, but sounded like the amazingly talented musician she also is—the front woman for a band that deserves success based on ability.

Hole is already hard at work on its next album, tentatively titled *Celebrity Skin*. It may include tunes they've debuted onstage, such as "Sugar Coma" and "Drown Soda" (the latter can be found on the Courtney-coordinated sound track to the movie *Tank Girl*), as well as a so-far untitled track with the lines, "He said, 'I'll never ever go away'/He said 'I'll always always stay.'"

In spite of the Kurt reference, perhaps Hole's third album will be the one that finally pulls the band away from the shadow of the valley of death—and into a musical nirvana all their own.

COURTNEY CONNECTIONS

CINEMA COURTNEY

Courtney Love has been acting her whole life: acting tough, acting cool, acting brash, brazen, and belligerent. Sometimes she pays for it; sometimes she gets paid. Courtney's screen appearances include bit parts in the Sex Pistols' saga, *Sid & Nancy*, a bigger role in the obscure *Straight to Hell*, and cameos in two upcoming movies: the Keanu Reeves film, *Feeling Minnesota*, as well as *Build a Fort, Set It on Fire*, about urban painter Jean-Michel Basquiat.

She's also featured in the documentary *Not Bad for a Girl*, on female-fronted alternative bands, screened at the 1995 L.A. Indie Film Festival.

WELL-CONNECTED COURTNEY

BILLY CORGAN, of Smashing Pumpkins, is an ex-boyfriend, and one of her closest confidants. "He kept me alive," Courtney confessed, of the roughest time after Kurt's death.

MICHAEL STIPE, main man for R.E.M., has been a real friend for a real long time.

EVAN DANDO, of the Lemonheads, was another who came through with comfort in the rough times— although, contrary to press reports, they were not romantically involved.

KIM GORDON, of Sonic Youth, produced Hole's first album.

KAT BJELLAND, of Babes in Toyland, was not only an ex-band mate, but posed on the collector's-item cover of "Retard Girl."

CONTEMPLATIVE COURTNEY

A once lapsed, now rededicated Buddhist, Courtney often retreats to the Namgyal Buddhist monastery and has met the Dalai Lama.

KURT'S COURTNEY

"He was my soul mate," she has said. And contrary to popular misconception, she wants it known that there was much that was normal about them as a couple—and as a family. "We ate breakfast, we ate lunch, we ate dinner, we rented movies, we ate ice cream, we played with Frances, we would read aloud to each other almost every night, and we prayed every night. We had some fucking dignity."

QUIPPABLE COURTNEY

"I found my inner bitch—and ran with her."

"Welcome to MTV Unglued."

"You should admit the embarrassing stuff—it makes you more vulnerable and it's cooler."

CONFOUNDING COURTNEY

Buried among her earliest musical inspirations: Karen Carpenter ("she had a really pure and beautiful voice and she soothed America for a decade," is Courtney's quote) and Stevie Nicks, who "represents the true California sound we are looking for."

COMMUNICATIVE COURTNEY

When she's not being tossed off the Internet, she routinely connects with fans via cyberspace. Check out the Hole forum (in Alternative Music) on America Online.

THE SPIRITUAL VOICE OF ALTERNATIVE

Live

CDs

Throwing Copper
(Radioactive Records) 1994

Mental Jewelry
(Radioactive) 1991

EP

Four Songs
(Radioactive) 1991

TEN-TRACK CASSETTE ALBUM
The Death of a Dictionary
(Action Front Records) 1989

76

PLAYERS Ed Kowalczyk vocals, guitar, songwriter
Chad Taylor guitar, vocals
Patrick Dahlheimer bass Chad Gracey drums

Throwing Copper took eight months to do it, but went to number 1 on *Billboard's* Top 200 Album chart. It has sold five million copies. "Lightning Crashes," the band's most commercial single, hit number 1 on the modern rock charts. "Selling the Drama," the first single to be released off *Throwing Copper*, was named Alternative Track of the Year by the trade publication *Radio & Records*.

HOW THEY GOT THEIR NAME

To know first: It rhymes with five, not give. To know next: They didn't have it until just before the release of *Mental Jewelry*—previously they were known publicly as Public Affection. It was during the recording of "Mirror Song" that Chad Gracey admitted his queasiness with their name. Alternate suggestions were placed in a hat: The one drawn was Live. The decision was sealed when later that night, Chad Taylor dreamed he saw a crew member wearing a hat emblazoned with the word *Live* on it.

OPERATION OVERNIGHT SUCCESS

If ever a band shot out of nowhere (York, Pennsylvania, close enough) to become the hippest, hottest, fastest—rising group on the planet, it's Live. *Throwing Copper*, only their second full—length album, has turned into precious metal.

What sets Live apart from other alternative bands is the power of ideas. Live gives you something to *think* about: Juliana may know how "Ugly" you're feeling; no one expresses rage better than Eddie Vedder; but fans walk away from a Live record fortified with nutritious brain food: hearty servings of songs about life, death, spirituality, and what you'd do if the world was ending tomorrow. And there's a multitude of reasons for their "overnight" success.

They're radioactive.

The name of their record company (a subsidiary of MCA), Radioactive, is also an apt description of how first alternative, then Top 40, radio has championed this band. The L.A.-based KROQ, widely credited with being the first and most influential alternative radio station in the country, half—jokingly calls Live their "house band."

They're MTVultures.

Every picture tells a story, and Live's lavish video landscapes are uncommonly moving visual narratives. The videos for "Operation Spirit" and especially "Lightning Crashes" broke the band as much as anything else did.

They treat each song reverentially.

Live's music is serious stuff, the absolute antithesis of, say, Green Day's flippancy. There's not a throwaway ditty in the bunch; each is a big serious song about a big serious issue.

They treat each member reverentially.

Yes, Ed is their feverishly intense lead singer slash lyricist slash philosopher. But Live is possibly the most democratic band in alternative music: Each member's contributions are given equal weight. From Chad Taylor's twangy guitar, to Patrick Dahlheimer's thick slick bass riffs, to Chad Gracey's robust percussion; all of Live is a collaborative effort. To reinforce that perception, each member does an equal amount of press. Just as many quotes fly from Patrick and the Chads as are well said from Ed.

Live's biggest concern echoes the refrain of so many of their alterna-peers: Can they survive commercial success and retain their alt credentials? Some

bands probably *should* worry; not Live: Music this profound and postures this gimmick-free won't soon stray into Bon Jovi-land. If Live has done nothing else, they have added yet another vibrant color to the alternative landscape. Besides, even though it appears their story is one of overnight success, it didn't happen quite so quickly. And it certainly didn't happen without a lot of training, support, pluck, dues-paying, and risk-taking.

FOUR ALONE IN SMALL TOWNE, U.S.A.
"There was nothing from the outside world—or inside—that could break us up." —Ed Kowalczyk

The members of Live may be unrelated in a biological sense, but they are very much family. The ties that bind are geographic, economic, philosophical, and emotional. They draw on the same bank of memories, influences, and experiences: They shared schoolrooms, teachers, confidences, flat Cokes, and days-old pizza. Most of all, they have always shared a passion for music—along with the keen sense of not fitting in.

Ed, Patrick, Chad T., and Chad G. grew up in semiindustrial, wholly patriotic York, Pennsylvania. While not exactly a cultural mecca, the town is known for some things: motorcycles, farming, and patriotism. Harley Davidson and Caterpillar (farming equipment) are the area's major employers; tourism is its most lucrative source of revenue. York was America's first capital during the Revolution, and these days, tourists arrive by the vanload to snap Polaroids of war fields and monuments. Chad, Ed, Patrick, and Chad didn't ride motorcycles; didn't farm (take that back, Chad T. *can* milk a cow), and saw only the cynical side of war.

Surely they weren't the only four outsiders in York, but they sure have stuck together. Live today is who Live has always been: None of the group has ever played in another band. Says Ed, "This band is really like a family in the sense that we grew up together, learned to play together—there was nothing from the outside world, or inside, that could break us up. It's like you can get into the biggest fight with your brother, but he's still gonna be your brother the next day."

Legend has it that these brothers-in-spirit started to play together out of boredom and in a garage, but like most legends, that's an oversimplification. They weren't bored so much as musically obsessed—and it was an attic, not a garage. These four were not just any listless small-town teens looking for something to do. They really were intrinsically talented,

ferociously dedicated, thoughtful, and hard-working.

They were also well trained. Patrick Dahlheimer and Chad Taylor took their first guitar lessons at Edgar Fahs Middle School. To this day, they credit Don Carn, "not your ordinary music teacher," for instructing them in the rudiments of their instruments, making them practice, and mostly, encouraging their budding passion for music.

Along with schoolmate Chad Gracey—who took lessons in jazz saxophone but is self-taught on drums—twelve-year-olds Patrick and Chad T. had started an instrumental group they called First Aid. They won several school talent shows;

it wasn't until the trio lost one that they decided to add a vocalist.

Ed Kowalczyk was a music student who hung around with them in Mr. Carn's classroom after school—enough reason to invite Ed to a rehearsal in the attic bedroom of Chad Gracey's house. Although Ed had long harbored dreams of singing, he hadn't done any before. "They kind of conned me into singing," Ed reminisced on a recent MTV special. "They said, 'Why don't you try singing for us?' So the first thing I sang with the band was Bryan Adams's 'Summer of '69,'" Ed remembers. They all remember that he wasn't great. "But it didn't matter," Patrick confessed. "We'd already decided that no matter what he sounded like, he was gonna be singing with us."

They all shared similar musical taste, nixing commercial pop for the more cutting edge Psychedelic Furs, Simple Minds, the Cure, and especially the passion and intellect of R.E.M., who were just blazing the first alternative trails. As Ed has recalled, "We were thirteen or fourteen years old, and just doing covers. . . . We attached ourselves to R.E.M. while learning to play our instruments. Me, in particular, because Michael Stipe has a baritone voice and I could sing those notes comfortably. And then once we started to write our own songs, that real gritty soulful quality in his voice and their music stuck with us to some degree."

With Ed aboard, the group changed its name to Action Front. They were determined to create their own music, based on their own experiences. Chad taught Ed guitar; the very first song they wrote together was called "Useless Moves." You won't find it on any Live recording; it was inspired by a fumbling romantic encounter in a school hallway.

By the time they entered William Penn Senior High School, they'd changed their name again, this time to Public Affection, and began playing at school dances and talent shows, from which they often walked away winners. While continuing to learn their instruments, they joined their school's marching band. "All the cute girls were in it, and we got to go on trips," admits Patrick, but at the end of the day, they got more out of it than they bargained for. "The marching band director, Harry Kehler, had a huge impact on us," says Chad Taylor. "I can remember being in a trumpet session and understanding crescendos and decrescendos. I still think that when I write guitar parts, I write trumpet parts."

Doing music had another unexpected bonus: It paved the way to peer acceptance at school. "In most schools, we would've been the geeks," Chad Gracey acknowledges, "but then we started with this band and people thought we were the coolest."

Although Ed, Chad, Patrick, and Chad were always serious about their music, they didn't consider it a viable career choice until one memorable night when they played at a gig that wasn't even theirs. During a dance at the local Temple Beth Israel, the hired band took a break. Public Affection impishly commandeered their instruments—and set the crowd on fire. "We just did the music everybody was just starting to listen to, the new-wave hits of the day—stuff by the Psychedelic Furs, R.E.M., Simple Minds, and the Cure. It went over huge, and people were freaking out," remembers Patrick. The display of public affection for Public Affection wasn't a fluke. The next time they were scheduled to play, over four hundred people paid four dollars a head to see them. With that, Chad Taylor declared, "This is going to be my career."

Word spread about Public Affection, which led to bookings. They played at various local clubs, the York YMCA, and the nearby Mercersburg Academy. The experience was priceless, but the pay stunk. Because the York-town boys weren't from wealthy families, all four had to work at part-time jobs while pursuing music *and* going to high school. Three worked at the same restaurant; Patrick clerked in a convenience store. There were times when it all seemed too much for one or another of them. "We used to pass notes to each other in study hall, pumping each other up," Ed says. "Saying, 'dude, we gotta do this band!'"

Local success notwithstanding, the collective decision to forego college and pursue their rock 'n' roll ambitions was a big-time roll of the dice. "We were the kind of guys that should have been headed for college," Chad Taylor says, "but we took a risk and went for the record deal instead. We were still living at home, we were still in our teens. It was scary."

Getting a professional booking agent to believe in them was the next logical step, but despite their local fame, they could not get anyone in a wider field to even give them a tumble. It took the intervention of Chad Taylor's dad to kick down that particular door. "Either you're going to listen to this band," he told an agent, "or you're going to make the biggest mistake of your life."

The agent, David Sestak, listened—and leaped into action. His advice was to prepare a demo to be shopped to indie labels and radio stations. Great advice—

but making a demo costs money. Renting studio time is expensive, as is pressing the actual record *and* promoting it. Confidence, talent, and gumption Live never lacked for; money was another story. They relied on intelligence and ingenuity to get what they needed.

It was Chad Taylor who first took the bull by the horns. "I decided that if you had to have money, you had to talk to people who knew how to get money *and* how to use it. My dad was a general contractor and I talked to his boss, who was the only millionaire I knew." Mr. Taylor's boss gave Live the idea to sell junk bonds—at one hundred dollars apiece—to finance their demo. Turned out to be a good idea. In 1989, they had the necessary funds and cut a ten-track cassette album. Titled *The Death of a Dictionary*, they pressed two thousand copies on their own Action Front Records and sold it at their gigs and local record stores. Only one of the songs on it, "Good Pain," made it onto *Mental Jewelry*.

With that, they were ready to rock from York to the bigger playground of New York. They focused on clubs where record company reps routinely scoured for new talent. "At first, nobody wanted to sign us," Chad Taylor told. "We have all these rejection letters up on the walls."

It was at the famous club CBGB's (Live has played there an estimated thirty times)

that Live got its first break. They got a demo deal from Giant Records, "which was big time for us," they said. The group worked with a Giant-assigned producer to record another demo, "but in the end, Giant passed—they dropped us." This time it didn't take long for another company to pick up the ball, however: After one last showcase at CBGB's, Radioactive Records nabbed the band. They were "handed" over to producer Jerry Harrison, ex-keyboard and guitar player for the Talking Heads, and the wheels were finally in motion. Live was alive—and about to kick butt.

MENTAL JEWELRY

While the name of the band is somewhat ambiguous, Live's music is not.

They're not often confused with any other band of any musical stripe. Perhaps there's a bit of R.E.M.'s folkie-tinged alternative, and some of Pearl Jam's metal muscle, but no other band on today's scene is as eerily spiritual or conjures up as much religious imagery outside, perhaps, contemporary Christian artists (which is kind of ironic, since Live's songs tend to question organized religion).

Few Live tracks are easy to decipher on first listen—in fact, most are so ethereal, cerebral, and dense, sometimes even the band members aren't totally sure what they're about. "I put complete trust in Ed to write the lyrics," admits drummer Chad. "I trust him enough that he's not going to write something completely controversial—but if he does, I'll stand up for it because he's also in my band. It's all one big circle with the band—he lets me play my drum part and I'll let him sing what he wants to." Chad Taylor agrees: "We express ourselves through our music, while Ed does it in words." Patrick adds, "We're all on the same train of thought."

That said, the main train of thought on their first major-label CD, *Mental Jewelry*, belonged to the Indian philosopher J. Krishnamurti. Ed happened across his writings while prowling a bookstore one day and remembers, "He had such an amazing impact on me that it affected everything we were doing as a band—so that planted a seed."

Among Krishnamurti's tenets was a questioning of our sources of knowledge and of organized religion. As opposed to relying on the strength of Gods and gurus, he championed instead self-responsibility, humility, and selflessness. What Ed got from it is this: "The answers to your problems are inside yourself—not in a God, or religion." Live called their album *Mental Jewelry* because "jewelry is something that people become attached to, mental jewelry is anything in your brain that you become attached to." Letting go of those attachments is part of Live's message.

Nowhere is that expressed better than in *Mental Jewelry*'s most famous song, the powerful and preachy "Operation Spirit (The Tyranny of Tradition)." "Heard a lot of talk about this Jesus/a man of love/a man of strength/but what a man was two thousand years ago/means nothing at all to me today," Ed howls, imploring the listener instead to "let it go!/Let it go!/Let it go my friend/And let's get it back/ let's get it back together."

Other songs on *Mental Jewelry* were odes to human kindness and brotherhood: "This ain't about no race, no creed," Live sang in "Brothers Unaware"—"You got ten fingers, two legs, one nose . . . like me, just like me." In "The Beauty of Gray," they espouse, "the perception that divides you from him is a lie . . . /this is not a black and white world/ . . . and I believe that maybe today we will all get to appreciate the Beauty of Gray." There were songs about world peace, "10,000 Years (Peace Is Now)," and inner peace, "You Are the World," as well.

Not surprisingly, some critics felt the band was too young to be tackling these "ideological rantings and ravings" and heavy issues. To some the record sounded more treatise than album tracks.

The worldly themes and less-than-hummable music didn't put much of a damper on *Mental Jewelry*'s success—it rose to number 73 on the charts and sold 480,000 copies. Which is, to put it mildly, not bad for anyone's debut album—and absolutely amazing for the York-town boys. "To be nineteen years old and from working-class backgrounds and suddenly be selling 400,000 copies of *Mental Jewelry* at a point when I didn't even *own* 10 records was pretty odd," Ed understated.

In fact it was mind-blowing. After touring in support of *Mental Jewelry*, Ed felt drained—and panicked. As he admitted on MTV, "I had no songs. I thought maybe we'd burned out, maybe there wouldn't even be a second Live album." It was practicality that conquered the panic. "We'd already rented studio time, and couldn't afford to lose it—so we went in. Chad suddenly started to play this amazing riff and that was it—we began again."

THROWING COPPER

"We haven't lost the passion and intensity of self-discovery, but this time we wanted to show more of our personalities." —Ed Kowalczyk

Don't look for hidden heavy-duty meaning in the name chosen for Live's second album. It has less to do with gurus, Gods, and philosophy than with BB guns. As per Chad, "Everyone thinks it's about throwing pennies, or some allusion to the song 'Waitress' (which puts down cheap customers), but it came about when Ed and Patrick got BB guns. Instead of using the expression 'throwing lead,' as if they were shooting at each other with real guns, they were saying, 'I'm throwing coppers at you.'"

Which could have been a signal that this new album was going to be less esoteric than the first—and in some ways it was. Rawer and looser than *Mental*, 1994's *Throwing Copper* became Live's breakthrough record.

Emotionally charged, it managed to be intimate and worldly at the same time. Like its musical predecessor, *Throwing*

Copper had its share of "big issue" songs. One track explores the search for inner peace ("Pillar of Davidson"); another forces conversation about the end of the world ("White, Discussion"); yet another—seemingly about a water hole the boys swam in as teenagers—includes a popular chant of the guru Baba Ram Dass (the line "be here now" is repeated in "Dam at Otter Creek").

The spiritual imagery that permeated *Mental Jewelry* reoccurs in *Throwing Copper*. Mentions of angels ("Lightning Crashes" and "All Over You"), death, the church, reincarnation ("I know, I know, I've been here before," on "Selling the Drama"), the garden of Eden ("I Alone") and Jesus are sprinkled throughout. Social commentary is alive and well also ("Shit Towne" and "Waitress").

But there are also songs about everyday life that marked a departure and artistic growth for Live. "We decided to take a look at where we came from—our town, our friends, our roots," explains Ed. They most obviously did just that in "Shit Towne," a song that's basically been done before—in their own ways—by Bruce Springsteen ("My Hometown"), Simon & Garfunkel ("My Little Town") and Juliana Hatfield ("Feeling Massachusetts").

On their track, Live explores their own "Shit Towne," putting the intended ironic spin on the poetic "good fences make good neighbors" provinciality of small town minds. In Live's version, "The Weavers live up the street from me/The

crackheads, they live down the street from me/we don't bother anyone, we keep to ourselves."

"Waitress" is a wry, witty, withering put-down of selfish patrons who can't see the human being behind the diner counter: They treat food servers like dirt. "She was a bitch, but she brought our food/everybody's good enough for some change," they argue, and—in a bow to Krishnamurti-type brotherhood again—"We all get the flu, we all get AIDS, we've got to stick together, everybody's good enough for some change/some FUCKING CHANGE!"

There are some relationship songs on *Throwing Copper*—but like all alternative love songs, they're more somber melodrama than lighthearted affairs of the heart. Ed admits, "Some of the songs come from having my heart broken—which really made me look inside myself." The compelling "All Over You," with its dynamic hook and angelic imagery, might be about the fluidity of love—how, like water, it can't be pinned down and held. "I Alone" expresses obsessive love, with references to Adam and Eve, the garden of Eden, and of course—the snake ("I alone tempt you"). For boys who follow the philosopher who eschews organized religion, their songs are full of traditional biblical references. All those years of Sunday school weren't lost on them.

"Selling the Drama" is another relationship song—this one about Live's ambiguous relationship with its growing audience. Edgy and moody and peppered with pounding guitar lines, "Selling the Drama" proffers, "It's the way we sing that makes 'em dream . . . and to Christ: a cross/and to me: a chair." Chad Gracey explains, "It's about the audience and the performer and how a lot of the time, the audience puts the performer up on this pedestal, and kind of almost worships him. But the song is about not playing into that ("And we won't be raped! And we won't be scarred by that!) and not taking advantage of it."

The defining song on *Throwing Copper*—what has become Live's signature song (or as they ruefully admit in concert, "our MTV song")—is "Lightning Crashes." Its commercial success (it hit number 1 on the *pop* charts) is partly due to the amazing hook, a chorus so catchy—"I can feel it comin' back again/like the rollin' thunder chasin' the wind"—that it grabs even those who've never heard of Live and don't particularly give a hoot what they're singing. Performed in "whisper-to-scream dynamics," "Lightning Crashes" gets more insistent with each verse; it is mesmerizing. Once it has crashed your consciousness, you can't get it out of your head.

Whether the millions who bought it care or not, part of the power of "Lightning Crashes" *is* its subject. It's about (apologies to Juliana) only everything: living and dying and the confusion in between. A few listens to the graphic lyrics tell of one life beginning ("a young mother cries/her placenta drops to the floor—the angel opens her eyes . . .") while another ends ("an old mother dies"). Both life and death are envisioned as an angel. The same angel who opened her "pale blue colored iris" in the first verse "closes her eyes" in the second—and in doing so transfers not so much her hopes and dreams to "the baby down the hall,"—but her confusion at life itself.

Confusion is what reigns when it comes to the song's interpretation: "Lightning Crashes" has been widely interpreted—and misinterpreted. Because of the dedication at the end to a friend who died at the age of twenty in a car accident, the assumption is the song was written for her. It wasn't—the dedication came after the song had been penned. Because of the video (ubiquitous on MTV), others have seen "Lightning Crashes" as an antiabortion tome; still others, a strictly life-affirming chant.

In *Spin*, Ed commented, "Nobody's dying in the act of childbirth, as some viewers think. What you're seeing is actually a happy ending based on a kind of transference of life." Lately, though, Ed has a new interpretation: "I thought this song was about living and dying; but now I think it's about rising and falling."

SELLING MORE DRAMA: THE FUTURE

"I think people are going to watch this band grow up." —Chad Taylor

A new album is already nipping at the heels of *Throwing Copper*; by mid-1995, the band had composed twenty-four new songs. Among the possibilities that will end up on the new record: "Freaks," which they've already performed in concert, and "Turn My Head," written by Ed for his current girlfriend.

Will a new Live be a different Live? While the next record promises to be lighter, "so we can survive," they half-joke, they don't think it'll be less weighty musically. In fact, Live exudes complete confidence in the power of their music—they always have. "We've known [we'd make it] all along—we know that our fifth or sixth or next record will be absolutely amazing. We will make a record that will be around for years and years—it's just part of the whole game plan," Ed once proclaimed.

But it would be a mistake to confuse confidence with conceit. For you'd be hard-pressed to find any in this band on a personal level. "I still think of us as this little band chugging away," says Patrick. Admits Chad Taylor: "I get scared when people call me a rock star; I just wanted people to like my music."

Ed is less concerned with the spoils of success. "We have a really strong foundation in our music and in our lives—it doesn't matter if we sell 100 or 100 million records." Chances are the future of Live lies somewhere in between.

LIVE WIRES

STAGE: Live has toured relentlessly since the release of their first album—and to those who've seen them, their name conveys the best way to appreciate them. "Each evening we wage war on our consciousness by pushing ourselves physically, emotionally, and spiritually. Every night we're trying to top the night before," Ed says.

MOST MEMORABLE GIG: Woodstock '94. "To play in front of 100,000 has to be the most intense rush I have ever experienced," says Patrick.

HOW A LIVE SONG GETS BORN: Chad Gracey explains the democratic system: "Someone always comes up with an initial idea. Ed may bring a whole story—melody, lyrics, verse, chorus—to us and we'll play it through." But that doesn't make it an instant track. "We'll either trash it or suggest things that could go here or there," Chad describes. Ironically for such a brainy band, the story often comes last. "A lot of times it's just syllables and nonsense to start with—no words, just sounds and a melody," Chad admits. But sooner or later, "what comes out the other end is a Live song."

SHINY, HAPPY PEOPLE: Because of the profundity and seriousness in their music, it has been widely assumed that the boys in the band are similarly intense, depressed, somber, haunted (take your pick of adjectives). To which they say nonsense. "Yes, we're serious onstage, but other than that, if you were to spend five minutes with us, we would blow that image out of the water. We're very happy." Ed puts it poignantly: "I never wake up and think that I could be more happy, you know? And that's rare in this world."

BAD TIMING AWARD: On the day *Throwing Copper* was released, Patrick's appendix burst—and as he recounted in Live's fan club newsletter, *Homespun*, "I celebrated by spending the day in the hospital on painkillers!"

VERY SERIOUS (INSPIRATIONAL) THOUGHT FROM ED, PRINTED IN *HOMESPUN*: On hearing of the suicide of Jeff Phillips, a skateboard artist who killed himself because he'd "lost hope," Ed wrote, "Having no hope can be a good thing. Hope takes you away from today and today is everything. I will never be one to oversimplify people's pain with too many words. I know pain can get thick. But when it gets thick, I just take a look around, call a friend, pick up a guitar and go into myself. Jeff Phillips, Kurt Cobain, and countless others are gone forever. This is our time. Tomorrow is today with a different name. Live now. Be free."

LIVE ON THE NET: America Online subscribers can access the Live message board under Rocklink . . . Alternative bands. Those who have Internet access can join the Live mailing list by sending e-mail to: Live-request   Mediafive.yyz.com.

OR JOIN THE FAN CLUB: "Everyone is invited to experience our passion," says Patrick. If you want to, it's Friends of Live, c/o Media Five Entertainment, 400 Northampton St., Easton, PA 18042. The (albeit sporadically published) newsletter is called *Homespun*. It's very Live.

Players

Trent Reznor vocals, guitar, songwriter

Chris Vrenna drums

Robin Finck guitar

Charlie Clouser keyboards

Danny Lohner keyboards, guitar, bass

Past Players

James Wolley keyboards

Richard Patrick guitar

Jeff War drums (deceased, 1993)

NINE INCH NAILS

CDs

The Downward Spiral (nothing/TVT/Interscope Records) 1994

Pretty Hate Machine (TVT/Formula Records) 1989

The Downward Spiral (nothing/TVT/Interscope) 1995

Fixed (nothing/TVT/Interscope) 1992

Further Down the Spiral (nothing/TVT/Interscope) 1992

Broken (nothing/TVT/Interscope) 1992

95

THE NAME GAME

What is known: Trent Reznor has been recording under that name since 1988—well before there was a band.

What isn't known: where it came from or what significance it has; whether it refers to something hammered, or some grotesque growth on the finger.

OVERVIEW

"There is no music out there like this. It is a step beyond."   —a fan

"Nine Inch Nails is not a real band with real people playing real instruments," states Trent Reznor, the man with the plan who is, always was, and forever will be the force behind Nine Inch Nails' visionary hammer. Instead, it is a concept, most often described as "industrial/computer rock" and more accurately as "bile-meets-the-groove music."

It is very different from anything else falling under the alternative umbrella. Trent is the antigrunge, all fishnet and eyeliner, as opposed (and he is) to flannel and denim. Nine Inch Nails—referred to by the devoted as simply "nin"—is a turbo-charged, snarling alternative to alternative.

Nine Inch Nails rages and rails against everything; theirs are songs of hatred, self-loathing, and despair. And they never scratch just the surface. The music cuts to the bone, and then deeper still. Characters don't just die in nin songs and videos; they are pummeled to death in meat grinders ("Happiness in Slavery"). They are never simply feeling blue, but usually suicidal ("Down in It").

It is all done with purpose and a clear vision: Trent's, who declared, "To me, rock music was never meant to be safe; I think there needs to be an element of intrigue, mystery, subversiveness. Your parents should hate it. If it pisses you off, that's great." The die-hards—and there are millions—understand. They relate to Trent as if he is the only one who truly understands the depths of their sorrow and loneliness.

It's not just what Nine Inch Nails is saying that separates it from other alternative bands: it's how the music is made—not by actual musicians playing in the studio, but by a one-man computer band, using software, sequencers, and sampling (borrowing snippets of other people's music—a few drum beats here; some keyboards there—and mixing them into their own songs). The combination of effects is powerful. Nine Inch Nails has hammered their way into the alternative mainstream with the darkest, most vicious, and most provocative sound around.

THE BECOMING
"I think the underlying basic thing is this: I've been superlonely." —Trent Reznor

What kind of warped individual could create the shocking, horrific images found between the nin grooves? There are two tempting views: Either Trent Reznor is a deeply disturbed psychotic who channels his inner demons into music, or he's simply a stagy shockmeister with a shtick. Both views, as it turns out, are distorted. The reality is more grounded *and* more complicated.

Trent knows his musical stuff: He's a classically trained piano prodigy. He knows his tech stuff: A self-professed computer dweeb, he studied computer engineering in college.

And the pathos comes from somewhere. He wasn't physically abused as a child, but felt "ripped off," and as he puts it: "For the record, YES, I've felt everything you hear in those songs. It's all real."

Michael Trent Reznor was born in the rural farming town of Mercer, Pennsylvania (outside of Pittsburgh), in May, 1965. When he was five, his parents, Nancy and Michael Sr., a commercial artist and amateur bluegrass musician, divorced—Trent was sent to live nearby with his grandparents. He started classical piano lessons and was quickly recognized as truly gifted.

He was also: a Boy Scout; a churchgoer; and a fishing buddy of his grandfather. He careened through the neighborhood on his skateboard and made model planes in his room. In addition to piano, he took lessons in sax and tuba. Teachers and school friends alike remember him as "quiet, polite, upbeat, friendly, popular, and very creative." His piano teacher didn't see the rage coming: He attested, "Trent's playing reminded me of Harry Connick, Jr." Trent took lead roles in his high school plays, *Jesus Christ Superstar* and *The Music Man*; he was voted "Best in Drama" by his classmates. Early photos show a neatly dressed, clean-cut, and handsome member of the Mercer Area Junior and Senior High School jazz and marching band.

What's wrong with this picture? As with any rendering from memory, everyone sees something different: It certainly isn't how Trent saw, or experienced, his childhood.

His home situation wasn't ideal, though Trent insists it wasn't totally awful. "I don't want to give the impression that it was a miserable childhood," he insists. Yet, he has given more than one hint that it wasn't great, either. Plagued with allergies—he had to wear a humiliating bathing cap swimming at the town pool— pathetically unathletic and often caught up in a fantasy world, he admits, "I always felt like a bit of a misfit. I just didn't belong. I don't know why. Looking back, it's like there was 'the club'—and I was always *almost* in there, but not quite."

He was not an academic superstar. Trent acknowledges, "If I wanted to get good grades, I could. But mostly, I didn't. I got a bad education because I had a bad attitude. Stuff I'd like to know now, at the time I thought was irrelevant. Typical teenage stupidity."

Trent's talent on the ivories was matched only by his passion for music. As his granddad, Bill Clark, told *People* magazine, "Music was his life, ever since he was a wee boy. He was so gifted." Unfortunately, being gifted musically did not win him popularity contests at school. "It wasn't cool to play music where I was from. If you were on the football team, you were a celebrity. If you were in a band, or took art class, like me, you were an outsider."

It wasn't as if he could stop playing: Music was just too important. "I was about thirteen when I realized I could express how I felt through a musical instrument," he remembers. His family wanted him to quit school, get a tutor, and become a concert pianist. But that was never in the cards for Trent. He discovered rock 'n' roll could better express what he felt, especially the music of Gene Simmons and KISS. "KISS was a big, early influence," Trent says. "If you could be like Gene Simmons, you had it made—girls, people would like you, you'd be famous."

From KISS, he graduated to Pink Floyd, but he was inspired more by artistry than any one artist. "It wasn't necessarily one genre, but they all had the common link of 'hey, I can relate to that.'" That idea stuck with him. Of his own music, later on, he'd say, "I just tried to address personal things that hopefully somebody else could relate to."

Whichever view is the more accurate—conventional insider or lonely outsider—it cannot be denied that Trent was, above all else, bored—and that would heavily influence the music he'd make later. "I don't know why I do these things, other than my desire to escape from Small Town, U.S.A., to dismiss boundaries, to explore. It wasn't a bad place where I grew up, but there was nothing going on but the cornfields. The rest of the world was a million miles away. It was like, you hear there's a world out there, but you can't get to it because you don't know where it is. My life experience came from TV, movies, books, and magazines. I was bombarded with images of things that seem cool, places that seem interesting, people who have jobs and careers and opportunities. None of that happened where I was. You're taught to realize it's not for you. It just instilled in me that I don't want to end up there."

His first foray out of Mercer was at Allegheny College. Trent enrolled as a computer engineering major, but hoped to minor in "fitting in and making friends." That didn't happen. Instead, he got even more immersed in music. At the time, a new sound was sweeping the college radio airwaves. It was music done, at least partly, by computer. Synth metal bands like Devo, Human League, and XTC were in the spotlight.

Trent was intrigued. "I liked technology and electronics. I liked the way it sounded . . . the idea that you could make a record with a machine. It was more interesting than guitar-bass-drum bands." Further, it all seemed do-able. "Synthesizers were becoming relatively affordable and sequencers for home computers were just coming out. And when I stumbled onto the harder-edged music that incorporated that, and the electronic elements, it pretty much fit with things that were already in my head. Suddenly, the music started to make sense."

The more sense it made, the less sense staying at school seemed to make. After a year, Trent left and headed for the nearest big city with a happening musical scene: Cleveland, Ohio.

There, he met drummer Chris Vrenna, and the two roomed together and got into the harder-edged sounds of '80s

metal bands Ministry and Skinny Puppy. Trent played with an endless series of bar bands, including his official "first," The Innocent. It wasn't the kind of music he wanted to make ("dinosaur AOR bullshit rock," he has termed it) and eventually, he didn't. When the band actually released its first album, "Livin' on the Streets," Trent was pictured on the cover, but never played a note on the record. "It was stupid. Dumb. Ridiculous."

Because money was scarce, Trent went the odd-job route. He kept close to the music business, however. He got a job as a handyman/janitor at Right Track Recording Studios, where he could observe and learn. During the day, he waxed floors and cleaned toilets; at night, he had the run of the place to himself. Trent put his all into both. As his former boss noted, "He was so focused, even when he waxed the floor, it looked great."

Of course, Trent had an agenda other than becoming the next Mr. Clean.

PRETTY HATE MACHINE
"It's the ultimate do-it-yourself record." —Karang (a British magazine)

The idea, of course, was to make a demo tape, even though he had no songs, no band, no actual knowledge of how to do it. But Trent was talented and driven and as he went about his janitorial chores, he watched, listened, and learned about the process of recording. Within a few months, he'd formulated a plan and was ready to give it a go.

As he's since described, "I realized the only way I was going to do this was by myself. I didn't have a band. The only means necessary was electronics. I came up with some rules and ideas—set up some parameters, and go! Musically, it was any instrument I'm going to use I'm going to play myself. So I had to learn bass and try to make an original sound on it, same with guitar." His proficiency on computers and all things technical served him well: He programmed all the music himself.

Writing proved a tougher challenge than instrumentation. "I always thought I could do it, but my greatest fear after all those years of dreaming about making music was to discover I didn't have anything to say. I was afraid of testing myself. I tried doing political stuff, like the Clash, but it seemed fake to me. So I started putting down how I felt inside, very private things—depressing things that you're not necessarily proud to say or that you want anyone else to hear. But it felt true."

The first song Trent ever wrote was "Down in It." An ironic fall-from-grace fantasy, it boasted spine-shifting rhythms and lyrics that went, "I used to be so big and strong/I used to know my right from wrong/I used to have something inside/Now just this hole that's open wide." It was a beginning.

Eventually, he had an entire album's worth of material—all done late at night by himself with Macs and mice.

Programmed electronically, the final mix meshed metal, synth, even disco and dance.

Working by himself had not made Trent a complete recluse: He'd made some human connections in the music world. One of them, John Malm, became not only his manager, but also the person who helped shop Trent's original demo to record labels. The response was mostly positive, but no one would sign him on the basis of a demo alone. Trent had to come up with a band and play live. "I had to find people who could understand where I was coming from," he explained, and who could faithfully—as faithfully as possible—recreate the sounds he'd made electronically in the studio. Or, as Trent would later say, "It's not about playing perfectly every night; it's about just understanding the message of the songs, whatever they might mean to you, and getting the point across."

He found what would be the first of many touring bands in roommate Chris Vrenna on drums, Richard Patrick on guitar, and Nik Rushe on keys. Several club dates later, they signed with the East Ccoast–based TVT Records, who gave Trent a tiny budget to make his record—and more importantly, complete creative control.

With all that, the record Trent made for TVT was not appreciably different from the demo they'd signed him on. A lot of what would be *Pretty Hate Machine* was done on a Macintosh computer, using a software program called Performer. As Trent described to *Musician* magazine, "Most of the keys were done on an E–Mix sampler along with a Prophet VS, Oberheim Expander and Mini Moog—all the drums and percussion stuff was done via sampler—stolen off other people's records! On this album I experimented a lot with looting other people's music—very subtly. Like taking a drum loop, and turning it around backwards and beginning it on beat two instead of beat one. You get this weird, syncopated rhythm. A lot of the time it sounds terrible, but sometimes, you get this incredibly complex percussion track where you didn't precisely program all the parts. Guitar-wise and bass-wise, it was some kind of Kramer, I couldn't really tell you what it is. That goes hand in hand with my guitar philosophy of knowing as little as possible about it."

What Trent eventually found to write about on *Pretty Hate Machine* was frustration, isolation, self-loathing, and obsession, both religious and sexual. Delivered through a thick sludge of gnashing guitars and computer-synthesized beats, it sounded like an industrial hate beat machine, with robotic dance rhythms and snatches of melody.

"Head Like a Hole" is the album's opening and most famous track. A disco-metal hybrid with furious, frenetic guitar riffs, it was both bleak and catchy. "Bow down before the one you serve/you're going to get what you deserve," Trent growled.

Pretty Hate Machine was released in 1989, was greeted unenthusiastically at first by radio, and went unembraced by the media, including MTV. Trent took his touring band on the road to promote it, and built a following with each gig. Smart misfits everywhere understood. Vengeful, masterful, hypnotic, it captured their anger, hostility, and alienation. The record became an underground hit and surfaced to eventually sell a million copies.

As nin's rep grew, they were added to the roster of the first Lollapalooza tour (in 1991) where they stole the show from would-be headliners Jane's Addiction. Nine Inch Nails had emerged from underground to become the happening industrial band on the alternative scene.

IF IT AIN'T "BROKEN . . ."

"I'm the lyrics. That's me. That gives enough of me away."
—Trent Reznor

Behind the scenes, things were not going well. There were record company hassles, and Trent's first impulse was to bolt. He didn't want to be under anyone's thumb. But he was no match for the legal system, and the contract he'd signed with TVT was nearly ironclad. It would take years to untangle the mess. Trent was determined, however, that he'd never make another record for them.

And he didn't. The next time he went into the studio, it was on the sly: TVT never knew he was working on a new album. It took three torturous years, but finally, there *was* a new nin record: Trent call it *Broken*. It was released through a combination of labels. TVT still had a stake in it, but after the legal battles were done, Nine Inch Nails was able to sign with Interscope as well as create their own label, called (lowercase) nothing records.

The battle for control of his music and of his career makes up *Broken*. "*Broken* is an ugly record," Trent confessed. "It was made during an ugly time in my life." In at least one track, he didn't even need lyrics to pound home his misery. "Help Me I Am in Hell" has been called a musical equivalent of Edgar Allan Poe's mystery "The Telltale Heart." The song starts with a single synth guitar line ticking like a clock. The tempo quickens and more clocks come in, until it seems as if the song will collapse under its rhythmic weight. Throughout in the background, a heartbeat is thumping slowly, like the sound of blood pounding in frightened ears.

"Happiness in Slavery" is the quintessential *Broken* song. The lyrics tell exactly how Trent felt about the record company battles. "I don't know where I've been/human junk/just words and so much skin. Stick my hands through the cage of this endless routine/Just some flesh caught in this big broken machine."

But it was the video, banned on MTV and nearly every other outlet, that caused the most ruckus. It took music video where few have dared to venture. One of the most graphically violent ever produced, it pictured a naked man being pulverized to death in a meat grinder.

Save for a few after-midnight local video shows, no one would play it; still, everyone talked about it. Trent insisted that "Happiness in Slavery" wasn't done for mere shock value. "We didn't set out to make the most vulgar thing we could just to get press . . . but it was a chance for me to finally be able to do something I wanted without having to ask someone [referring to record company flacks] who has no fucking idea. Besides, these were

the most appropriate visuals for the song," he said matter-of-factly.

The fact of the matter was *Broken*, in spite *or* because of its unadulterated outrage and outrageousness, went on to win a Grammy Award for its artistry. On its heels, Trent went ahead and remixed many of the tracks, released as the EP *Fixed*.

THE DOWNWARD SPIRAL
"It's the darkest album ever to crack the national Top 10." —*Los Angeles Times*

Many nin fans believe that only when Trent is mired in the depths of despair can he make the kind of music they hope for and respond to. They got just what they wanted in 1994. As Trent told *Spin*, "At this point in my life I'd gotten everything I ever wanted, but it didn't seem to be what I wanted. And I start thinking . . . why do I feel this way? What's all this negativity about? This anger? Why am I so self-destructive? I wanted to write about someone who was decaying, someone who was looking for salvation or hope through dangerous and improper means." What he came up with was his second full-length CD, *The Downward Spiral*.

A concept album about one man's descent into suicidal depression, *Rolling Stone* called it "existential pain expressed as rock 'n' roll." Trent saw it a little differently: "It's about somebody discarding parts of themselves, religion, love, caring about the opinions of others—ultimately for self-realization."

In the misery arena, Trent was in rare form: The album was even recorded in the house where the most notorious crime of the century—the 1969 Sharon Tate murder committed by the Manson cult—had occurred.

First out of the pen was "Mr. Self-Destruct," an anguished cry for something to believe in at a time when all the old standbys—government, religion, family—no longer provide answers. Trent growls, "I am the voice inside your head—and I control you/I take you where you want to go—and I control you/I give you all you need to know—and I control you/I drag you down and use you up/Mr. Self-Destruct."

Further down the musical spiral, on "I Do Not Want This," he barks, "Don't you tell me how I feel/you don't know just how I feel." On "Hurt," the despair is palpable: "I hurt myself today to see if I still feel the pain."

The title track is a suicidal description set to music written when Trent really was "superdepressed." One verse goes, "He couldn't believe how easy it was/he put the gun to his face." Naturally, lyrics like those lead to charges that Nine Inch Nails is promoting death by one's own hand. Trent sees it just the opposite way. "I've thought about it, but I've found that saying it—singing about it—almost demystifies it."

What happened to make Trent spiral out of control this time? Many pinpoint the death of his dog, Maise. Trent-observers believe the canine was his closest-to-human connection in the entire world. Rock's master of darkness does seem to walk the anguished walk as well as he talks the talk: Trent is reclusive, has few friends or

attachments. "I don't trust people very much," he has admitted. "I don't like that many people." Some say he's as cold and hard as a nail. But when his dog died, he went into seclusion; years later, he's still dealing with the grief.

Whatever propelled Trent toward his personal downward spiral, millions of fans followed willingly: The record crashed out of the gate at number 2 on the Top Album charts its first week. It went on to multiplatinum status.

On a personal level, Trent confessed that finishing the album made him feel as though "a weight has been lifted." He felt good enough, too, to remix eleven of its tracks and release an EP called *Further Down the Spiral*, which successfully spiraled up the record charts.

ON WITH THE SHOW!

Nine Inch Nails has always toured incessantly, albeit with a revolving door of players. "For each tour, I pick players best suited to the range of attitude and musical taste to translate the material into a live show," Trent tells.

A show is what fans get, with plenty of eye-candy. Onstage, Trent is an androgynous vision in black leather. He wears thick, smeared eyeliner, fishnet stockings, garter belts. It is all done for maximum effect, as Trent declares, "When I go see a show, I want to see freaks, dancing midgets, flesh and blood. I want icon and entertainment." And in a swipe at grunge, he adds, "Turning the whole thing into rock theater is more

interesting to me than watching five guys dressed like gas station attendants with their heads down." The splash of glam provided by Nine Inch Nails is not without pure rock roots: Alice Cooper, Adam Ant, David Bowie, Jim Morrison, and most especially, Trent's boyhood idols, KISS, all did it before.

Surrounded by smoke machines and strobe lights, Trent is a model of hyperathleticism. But amid the carefully choreographed chaos, he also manages to display raw, emotional vulnerability. "Every night I'm saying the most personal thing I could ever say," Trent relates. "But one of the prices is that there's a raw nerve I'm letting everybody look at."

They don't only look, of course. Audiences sing, sweat, and rage along with the celebration of hate and self-loathing. Which still feels strange to Trent. "It's a bizarre feeling to be in front of people you've never seen before, will never see again, and they're singing words back to you that came from inside—and they look like they mean it. And they have no idea what I am talking about, but it means something to them and that's cool."

By night's end, it's more than cool. Emotional slates are wiped clean. As any fan will attest, a Nine Inch Nails concert is a draining and exhilarating experience, complete catharsis and self-purification for its creator and for its fans. Trent bleeds; fans heal. That, perhaps more than anything else, is the ultimate strength and power of

TRENT'S TRUE CONFESSIONS

ON VIDEOS:

"I see music video as an art form that could have turned out pretty cool, but due to the powers at MTV, it turned into nothing but a business of three-minute commercials for the public to be told what to buy and what to like."

ON HIMSELF:

"I'm just a bummed-out guy from Cleveland with a death band."

ON THE FANS:

"They're the most important thing there is."

ON THE DARK SIDE:

"I've hit lows in my life, but fortunately, it hasn't involved . . . bottoming out."

THE LIGHT SIDE:

He checks into hotels under various aliases, including the names of '70s TV star Randolph Mantooth (*Emergency*) and the Six Million Dollar Man, Steve Austin.

ON COOL:

"It's not up to me to stand at the door and say, 'You are cool, you can come in, but you aren't cool, so stay away.' Under those rules I never would have been allowed in. When I was growing up, I was never one of the kids that anyone called 'cool.' That's where a lot of the anger started."

ON LOVE & HAPPINESS:

"I do have the capacity to love. I have loved—and I mean, truly loved—several times. I'm not afraid of it. Happiness, and trying to sustain it for any length of time, that's where the trickery lies."

ON FUTURE NAILS:

"I am not out to change the world. I want to make quality music and keep doing things that are challenging to me."

SIDE PROJECTS:

"The most famous is coordinating and contributing to the sound track of Oliver Stone's movie *Natural Born Killers*. To come, there's a collaboration with '80s glam icon Adam Ant—with whom he sometimes duets on stage—in the movie *Full Dead Drop*.

IN CYBERSPACE:

It's more than fitting that a computer-driven band can be reached via cyberspace. There are several web sites along the internet. Try these: http://www.scri.fus.edu/ patters/nin.html.

Pearl Jam

THE REBELLION OF ALTERNATIVE

PLAYERS

EDDIE VEDDER vocals

STONE GOSSARD guitar

JEFF AMENT bass

MIKE McCREADY guitar

JACK IRONS drums (as of 1995)

PAST PLAYERS

DAVE ABBRUZZESE drums (on Vs. and Vitalogy)

DAVE KRUSEN drums (Ten)

CDs

Vitalogy (Epic Records) 1994

Vs. (Epic) 1993

Ten (Epic) 1992

EP

Alive (Epic) 1991

Ten sold about that many copies when it was first released. Now, it's up to nine million, that is, as of the summer of 1995. It continues to rack up sales. *Vs.* made rock history for having the "biggest debut of all time." The first week it was available, it sold 950,000 copies. It has topped the five million mark. *Vitalogy* has sold five million copies since it came out in November 1994. It, too, made history its debut week—selling 877,000 copies right out of the gate, second only to *Vs.* Both *Vs.* and *Vitalogy* made their amazing debuts without the benefit of singles, marketing, promotion, or videos.

Pearl Jam

ABOUT THEIR NAME

In 1991, when Eddie Vedder was first summoned to Seattle, he was hoping to join a band called Mookie Blaylock, which included Stone, Jeff, Mike, and Dave. But a few months later, when the five signed with Epic and rush-released the EP *Alive*, they were Pearl Jam—for Eddie's Grandma Pearl and her quite amazing homemade jam.

REARVIEWMIRROR

Pearl Jam got to be the world's most popular rock band by doing everything in their power to avoid becoming the world's most popular rock band. Everything, that is, except unleash powerful, raw, emotional music that instantly grabs listeners by the gut, inspires, uplifts, and—as countless fans have testified—even saves lives. But you won't hear the music marketed on the radio in any sort of traditional way—Pearl Jam doesn't release singles. You won't read many quotes by band members in the mainstream press: Pearl Jam rarely does interviews. You won't see them performing on MTV: Pearl Jam stopped doing videos three years ago. And it has become increasingly difficult—bordering on impossible—to see this band live: Their last two scheduled tours have mostly crashed and burned amid a morass of sticky ticket controversies.

Pearl Jam has forged an against-the-grain image to the max. They are steadfastly against everything the least bit commercial. Yet commercial success is what they've achieved—to the max. They've not sold *out,* but they *have* sold, more records worldwide, than any other alternative band.

The not-so-secret recipe to Pearl Jam's success is the music, raw, pure, and raging. It's music that mixes the first person painful with third person political, powered by a passion that energizes and stirs the soul. Starting out with searing songs like "Alive," "Jeremy," and "Black," Pearl Jam was one of the first alternative bands to reflect a new generation's alienation and anger. They were one of the first and biggest to bring alternative into the spotlight from underground to world prominence. Made in Seattle, they (along with Nirvana) *made* Seattle the grunge capital of the world. And they're one of the originals who continue to inspire passion, fierce loyalty, and megamillions in sales, courtesy of their rabid fans.

The crunching, brash, and beautiful contributions of the instrumentalists notwithstanding, perhaps the most potent part of Pearl Jam is its lyricist and vocalist, the much-maligned/much-revered Eddie Vedder. As *Rolling Stone* once put it, "A lot of singers know how to convey emotion in a song, but few are capable of the kind of range or drama that Vedder routinely imparts. There's enough power and desperation in his voice to move you even if you don't hear or understand or even much care about the words." Yet there's no fan who doesn't get it. And that is the magic of Pearl Jam: Since its official inception in 1991, it has by turns cradled, nurtured, expressed the feelings of, and fought like hell for its fans.

In their first self-scrawled press release—back in those innocent *Ten* days—the band wrote, "The Journey Begins. Like your favorite plant, just add water. Watch Pearl Jam grow."

ONCE

Pearl Jam is often lambasted by the self-proclaimed alt-police for not *really* being alternative. It's not that they're huge—so are R.E.M. and Green Day—but unlike those, Pearl Jam was never small; they didn't even start out on an independent label. *Ten* debuted on the very corporate Epic, a division of Sony. But what the indie purists forget is that Pearl Jam's roots are as deeply, authentically alternative as you get.

In its embryonic stage, Pearl Jam was Montana—born bass player Jeff Ament and Seattle guitarist/songwriter Stone Gossard. In 1985, along with guitarist Steve Turner and singer Mark Arm, they were part of the hard-rocking grunge pioneers Green River, specializing in big-riff, garage-style guitar rock. Their first EP, "Come On Down," was released on the small, independent Homestead Records. A year later, the band signed with Subpop—the indie label responsible for Nirvana, which would go down in history as the icon of grunge indie labels. On Subpop, Green River rolled with two CDs, "Dry as a Bone," in 1987, and "Rehab Doll," in 1988.

Green River forked into several tributaries. Steve Turner and Mark Arm left to form Mudhoney. They stayed with Subpop, but the others didn't; as L.A.-based major labels had just discovered the alternative scene and swooped down on Seattle to raid the little labels of their talent. Stone and Jeff, who'd hooked up with singer Andrew Wood to form Mother Love Bone, were the recipients of that first wave of major label largesse. They signed with Polygram Records. In 1990, Mother Love Bone released what would be its only album. The bluesy, hard-rocking *Apple* came out just after Andrew's untimely drug-related death.

Wracked with grief, the surviving members splintered, but played on. Jeff jammed briefly with War Babies, but spent most of his time on his other passion, graphic arts. Stone alone began composing new music. Among his compositions was a hard-driving riff he called "Dollar Short." Late in 1990, he determined to pull a new band together. He recruited explosive lead guitarist Mike McCready, a veteran of the defunct Seattle band Shadow. Stone then lured Jeff back into the fold and secured the percussive services of one Dave Krusen—which left the slot of lead singer open.

EDDIE: ROCK'S "VOICE OF DYSFUNCTION"

Eddie Mueller grew up— miserable and misunderstood—in Evanston, Illinois. The oldest of four, he was raised by his mother and an abusive man he believed to be his father. In his teen years, he moved with his family to San Diego, where he spent hours alone in his room

playing guitar and listening to rock— especially The Who's *Quadrophenia*. Later, he'd admit that Pete Townsend's power chords were what kept him going. "Music is a very powerful art form. You've got words and music and volume—it's not just the way the chords can move that can uplift you, but you can turn this thing up loud. Live, it can be so loud it shakes your chest. It can be very emotional. The only thing that was actually positive in the old days was getting to see a band I liked."

In most other aspects of young Eddie's

life, negativity—and deceit—ruled. When his family decided to return to the midwest, Eddie stayed behind, mostly to escape the beatings of the man who'd raised him. One day his mom flew back to San Diego with the startling news bulletin that would eke its way into his music a few short years later: Not only was her abusive husband not Eddie's real father, but the man who *was*—a "family friend"—lay dying of multiple sclerosis. Eddie would never get the chance to forge a bond with his biological father. "I spent my life with fucking lies," he'd rage.

In quick succession, Eddie dropped his stepfather's surname, adopted Vedder (his mother's maiden name), quit high school, spent his days pumping gas and surfing, his nights jamming with various bands and filling journals with original music. Intense, edgy, and immersed in the San Diego music scene, he was known as "the guy who never slept." Through the grunge-vine, he befriended another music scene vet, ex–Red Hot Chili Peppers drummer, Jack Irons. It was he who provided Eddie with the link to what would become Pearl Jam. For Jack had gotten hold of a five-track cassette of instrumentals, dubbed "Stone Gossard Demos, 1991." He gave it to Eddie: Listening changed the young man's life.

"I played it at work, all night, and then went out surfing," Eddie remembers. "It was a great feeling: a combination of sleep deprivation and being very excited by the coldness of the water—with this music floating around in my head." He was especially intrigued by the tune "with the great bridge." It was the one Stone called "Dollar Short."

Within hours, words to go along with the tunes were floating onto paper—lots of it. Quickly scribbling lyrics on yellow Post-Its, Eddie made a tape of himself singing them over Stone's guitar throws. Together, there were three songs that told a story—they were "Alive," "Once," and "Footsteps." He even designed some graphics to complete the tapes—and mailed them to the Seattle address of Jeff Ament.

"Stone, you better get over here," are the by-now legendary words all Pearl Jam fans know. For as soon as Jeff heard Eddie on the tapes, *he* knew: This was something amazing. And it only comes around once in a musical lifetime.

Eddie flew to Seattle, settled into the basement of an art gallery, and began rehearsing with Jeff, Stone, Mike, and Dave. They'd been calling themselves Mookie Blaylock, but soon after Eddie's arrival, changed it—ostensibly to honor his grandma Pearl's unusual jam. Creativity flowed: Song after song poured forth from the combo, more than enough for an entire CD, let alone the three-track EP promo sampler "Alive," which was first released in 1991. For the already pedigreed band snared a contract with alternative-hungry Epic Records almost immediately.

On the heels of the "Alive" EP came the CD *Ten*.

THE COMING TOGETHER OF *TEN*...
HANDS, EYES, EARS
"When we were writing the songs, I had no idea that so many people would relate." —Eddie Vedder

Ten was all earnest musical muscle, a collection of eleven midtempo songs revolving around loss, alienation, and suicidal insanity. Few rhymed, as life doesn't often fit neatly into iambic pentameter. Arguably the most shocking song on *Ten* is the one that started life as the Stone-riff, "Dollar Short." Eddie, of course, redubbed it "Alive." Sad and grating, "Alive" is often (mis)interpreted as a life-affirming song. Only in later interviews did fans learn that it is instead a chronicle of Eddie's torment, his anguished reaction to the deceit he lived with, and the crushing confusion the truth brought. "Alive" is about the day Eddie learned of his real father.

The lyrics are painfully transparent. "The story of the song is that a mother is with a father and the father dies," Eddie recounted in *Rolling Stone*. "It's an intense thing because the son looks just like the father. The son grows up to *be* the father—the person that she lost. His father's dead, and now this confusion. The mother loved the father, and the resemblance to the son is uncanny. But the son is oblivious—he doesn't know what's going on. He's still dealing with the death of his father. All he knows is 'I'm still alive.' And those three words—that's totally out of burden. Because he's not sure he deserves to be. He doesn't know what to do with it."

What Eddie did with it is continue the story in two more songs—one of which, "Once," opens *Ten*. In that haunting, eerie track, the same tormented boy who

"Once . . . upon a time, could control [himself]" becomes a serial killer. In the final part of the trilogy, "Footsteps," which was released as a single in England, he gets caught and executed. Eddie quips, "My folks, they've given me a lifetime's worth of material. . . . I'm just glad I became a writer."

Still, the writing can deliver brutal emotional blows. Five years later, "Alive" still tortures its author. Reflecting on it, he admitted, "There are certain songs that come from emotion, it's got nothing to do with melody, or timing, or even words; it has to do with the emotion behind the song. You have to sing them from a feeling. 'Alive,' and 'Jeremy,' and 'Black,' these songs, they tear me up."

In his allusion to the power of *Ten*'s most famous song, "Jeremy," Eddie is hardly alone. Chilling and emotionally complex, it reaches deep into the psyche of anyone who's ever been bullied at school or did the bullying. For the song is told from the perspective of both. "Jeremy," of course, is the story of the long-neglected outcast who freaks out in class one day, lashing out at his tormentors: "hit me with a surprise left, my jaw left hurtin"; his parents: "Daddy didn't give attention to the fact that mommy didn't care"; and finally at himself. "Jeremy spoke in class today," Eddie wails over and over. And his long-suppressed rage won't soon be erased from memory. "Try to erase this from the blackboard," Eddie demands.

Of course, *Ten* wasn't only about lyrics. The music was raw, ragged, and in-your-face; it cut with hard-driving buzz saw guitar riffs. In what would become Pearl Jam's trademark, all the songs built "from the bottom up": first, the drums, then bass, and then the layers of guitars, and finally vocals.

CAN'T FIND A BIGGER BAND—EXCEPT (FOR A WHILE) NIRVANA

"When you sit in your room and play guitar, [being a huge rock star] is just not what you're thinking about—at least it wasn't what I was thinking about." —Eddie Vedder

Ten was titled so because—as the boys had written in that earliest press release—it was "the coming together of 10 . . . hands . . . eyes . . . ears." When it first came out, Eddie hoped it would sell "something like 40,000 copies." Seemed like an optimistic figure. And in contrast to the songs, the band's mood was *upbeat* and optimistic when *Ten* was released—an unusual collective emotional state and one that would not be repeated any time soon. Partly it was the time and the place it was all happening, which combined, would once and forever connect Pearl Jam with those other Seattle-scene grunge-icons, Nirvana.

The two bands were compared and contrasted from the start—and in 1991, Pearl Jam was stuck at the bottom of the hipper-than-thou polls, while Nirvana, courtesy of their single "Smells Like Teen Spirit" from their major label debut album, *Nevermind*, rose to an exalted spot on the hip-parade. *Ten* languished while *Nevermind* flourished; Pearl Jam's hard-rock sound was immediately dubbed as a rip-off and not alternative. To the self-proclaimed alt purists, Kurt Cobain and his band were the real thing; Pearl Jam were impostors.

Kurt exacerbated the conflict, lashing out at "Eddie Bedwetter" and his band of copycat retro rockers, saying, "I find it offensive to be lumped in with Pearl Jam . . . They were never part of the underground." Eddie, who didn't always keep his thoughts to himself, actually half-agreed on that last point with Kurt.

Eventually, the spat between the supergroups was patched; unfortunately, the grudge match would end tragically when Kurt took his own life a few short years later. But even before that, slow starter *Ten* went on to outsell *Nevermind*, and Pearl Jam got huge; the video for "Jeremy" was all over MTV. Eddie, whose face was plastered all over the covers of both the music and the general press, was hailed as one of the first alternative rock Gods. All of which he hated. And all of which he rails against to this day. But nothing could stop this train. Pearl Jam went on to expand the boundaries of alternative rock and create some of the most powerful, timeless, and for some, life-sustaining, music ever. One year after *Ten*, came *Vs*.

FIVE *Vs*. . . . WELL, JUST ABOUT EVERYTHING, EXCEPT GREAT MUSIC

"I may be shy about some things, but not when it comes to the music. Someone has to stick up for the music." —Eddie Vedder

Up to the day of its scheduled release, Pearl Jam couldn't agree on what to call it—and the record company couldn't wait around. So the very first pressing of the second album—which hundreds of thousands waited on line the day of its release to buy—pictured a wild animal breaking free of its cage on the cover, and went simply by *Pearl Jam*. In fact, what was just about to be *Five Vs. One* eventually was simply *Vs.* That would be pronounced *versus*, meaning "against."

It was only one year after *Ten*, but clearly the band had grown more confident. If *Ten* was full of turbulent, sad, and somber songs, *Vs.* was, as a whole, a whole lot angrier—it was also harder, faster, and meant to be played louder. The songs were more diverse, as Pearl Jam's repertoire had expanded to include songs that told stories, songs from a woman's point of view, songs with a political message, and one that even poked fun (fun! what a novel concept for Pearl Jam!) at the King of Pop himself, Michael Jackson. Another notable change: Drummer Dave Krusen was long gone (leaving "for personal reasons") and had been replaced by Dave number two: this one, Abbruzzese, of Houston, Texas.

Musically, *Vs.* presented the band as a more cohesive unit. One reviewer aptly described it as a combination of "crunching and melodic, raw and graceful, mystical and visceral, brash and beautiful." Layered with guitars and strong percussion, the tunes once again built from the bottom up and carried the power of heavy metal combined with the flavoring of great pop. Some songs seemed catchier than those on *Ten*—but not a one was less emotionally complex. And this time, the music on each cut matched the lyrical mood perfectly.

The funk-edged tribal beats of the antiracism song "W.M.A." echoed the savage scenario of police brutality against an African-American. (The song was about an actual crime against a man named Malice Green, who was beaten to death by Detroit police—and whose photo appears in the liner notes of *Vs.*)

"Animal," with its punchy power chords and feral slurring, continued the antiviolence theme, bemoaning the lack of kindness among humans and the mindlessness of brutality. "I'd rather be with an animal," Eddie snarls.

The specific animal alluded to in "Rats" takes it even further—'cause, as Eddie notes, rats, "don't scab . . . don't fight . . . don't oppress an equal's given right." The song, which could have come off as preachy, is absolved by Eddie's earnest snarls—and by the sly tinge of humor at the end, when Ed tweaks Michael Jackson's rat-as-best-friend song, intoning, "Ben, the two of us need look no more . . ."

The riff-driven rocker "Rearviewmirror"

recounted the suicidal ruminations of an abused (like Eddie?) boy running from the pain in his past. "I took a drive today/time to emancipate/I guess it was the beatings/made me wise/tried to endure what I could not forgive," is the chorus. The narrator in "Indifference" is similarly abused: "I yell until my lungs give out, but what difference will it make? I'll keep taking punches until their will grows tired."

Abuse comes up again in "Go"—which seems to chronicle domestic husband vs. wife violence—and contains the threatening line, "suppose I abused you/just passing it on."

Perhaps the most famous song on *Vs.* is the acoustic "Daughter," told in spooky, disjointed prose about an anguished little girl who is being held down—and probably sexually abused when "the shades go down." "Don't call me daughter . . . not fit to," Eddie sings. "Daughter" became a pro-choice anthem when sung live at a Voters for Choice concert in Washington, D.C., last year. During that show, Eddie added the lines, "My body's nobody's but mine/you have your own body/let me have mine."

The title *Vs.* should have made the corporate music industry take heed:

Pearl Jam was about to take a stand against anything and everything that smacked of marketing and commercialism.

The band as a whole was freaked by the runaway success of *Ten*. Personally, Eddie was cowed by it. "As the audience gets bigger, I get smaller," he once confided. There was the fear that the unwanted attention might corrupt the music, or worse, the very concept of alternative. For being huge meant being mainstream and corporate: exactly what they were an alternative *to*.

Pearl Jam proclaimed that *Vs.* would spin off neither radio-ready singles nor videos. Despite (or maybe because of) the success of the video for "Jeremy," Eddie said, "I just don't put any weight into those things, I have a hard time caring about it." Jeff was influenced by a rocker friend who hated the "Jeremy" video—because it spoiled his own mental picture of the song.

Additionally, there would be no rounds of press interviews or photo sessions—no marketing ploys at all for *Vs.* The music would live or die by just that.

It lived. And flourished. And basked in brilliant reviews. The music press canonized it; the you-don't-get-more-establishment than *Newsweek* magazine called it "an absolutely first-rate rock 'n' roll album." And like *Ten*, it went on to multiplatinum sales; like *Ten*, too, it went on to be compared with Nirvana's sophomore release, *In Utero*. It outsold that one also.

The one thing Pearl Jam was *for* vis-à-vis *Vs.* was playing the music live for their fans—who waited on line and with bated breath for the chance to be where Pearl Jam was, to feel and experience the power of music so close it "shakes your chest," as Eddie once said.

Live is where Pearl Jam does it best; live is where Eddie runs on pure instinct, growling, wailing, chanting, murmuring: his finger on the pulse of the crowd's collective surging emotions. And his own. "In order to sing our songs," Ed said, "they have to be felt. And it's a tremendous privilege to be able to play music for a bunch of people. It's a great feeling, very humbling."

Pearl Jam had toured for *Ten* and had performed at 1992's Lollapalooza festival, where tales of Eddie's corkscrew moves and fiery passion onstage became legendary. *Vs.* was released at the end of 1993 and plans had been afoot for an extensive summer '94 tour. But that's when Pearl Jam came up against what would prove an immovable corporate object: Ticketmaster.

RAGE AGAINST THE MACHINE
"The struggle is everything. The push and pull is what makes our band." —Jeff Ament

For all the power of Pearl Jam's music, they risk becoming better known for their politics. They took a very public stand versus marketing and commercialism. They professed not to care if that hampered music sales (it didn't). But they painted themselves into a corner when they took up arms against the conglomerate ticketing agency Ticketmaster: No way could either retreat or surrender. Pearl Jam might have ended up being the champions of reform in the tour business—or martyrs of a failed grassroots rebellion. As of the moment, it's the latter.

Much ink has flowed regarding the Pearl Jam–Ticketmaster combat. In spoon-size biblical bites, it was about the righteous David (Pearl Jam) going up against the greedy giant Goliath (that would be Ticketmaster). Only this time, the rock(ers) didn't fell the bad guy.

Ticketmaster is the agency that sells tickets to live entertainment—including rock concerts—over the phone, by computer. It's a convenient way fans can get tickets without going to the venue itself and standing on line. For the service, Ticketmaster tacks a surcharge onto the price of each ticket. Which wasn't the problem per se—it was the amount they were charging, which could go from three to fifteen dollars. Pearl Jam wanted to keep ticket prices to their shows down to an affordable twenty dollars, surcharge included. As Eddie explained, "We don't want to exclude anyone from the experience . . . the experience of a father taking his son to the concert even if he works at a gas station—or being able to afford a T-shirt. What music can do to your life, what one night of live music—who knows what it can do?"

The members of Pearl Jam and their crew had agreed to a cut in personal salary to make the tour happen at an affordable price for their fans. But Ticketmaster, which had compromised its prices somewhat for other bands, could not reach an accord with this band. The bigger problem turned out to be the lack of viable alternatives for the kings of alt rock: Ticketmaster had exclusive contracts with most of the venues at which Pearl Jam was scheduled to play. In other words: If they couldn't or wouldn't use Ticketmaster, they couldn't play at most of the appropriate venues across the U.S.A.

Pearl Jam—who, it should be noted, were not supported in any real way by other bands (they got lip service from R.E.M., but no one canceled Ticketmaster tours in solidarity)—refused to cave. They took their fight all the way to the U.S. Justice Department, accusing Ticketmaster of unfair monopolistic policies. Stone and Jeff testified in court; an official government investigation ensued. A year later, Ticketmaster emerged victorious; they were found innocent of any legal wrongdoing.

Later, Pearl Jam tried an alternative tack, signing up the following year with another ticketing company, ETM, who promised a not-higher-than $2.45 surcharge for tickets. But insurmountable problems ensued. Aside from the out-of-the-way venues ETM could do business with (in Casper, Wyoming, for instance)—since Ticketmaster had the big ones—it turned out that Pearl Jam was ETM's . . . uh . . . first big customer. And the glitches in the system were overwhelming. The alternative tour did start—but didn't get far. It was plagued with problems, only some of which had to do with the baby agency.

Pearl Jam's fans were the ones who lost big time. For the battle ended up scuttling not one, but two tours. The *Vs.* tour never happened; the one for their next album, *Vitalogy*, started then sputtered, then started again.

VITALOGY
"We are just still being brutally honest and giving it our best." —Eddie Vedder

If they weren't touring, they were working on new material, and Pearl Jam's third CD, *Vitalogy*, came out in November, 1994, exactly one year after *Vs.* It moved the band into more experimental musical waters; only some of which, it must be said, were lapped up by die-hard fans. *Vitalogy* pulsed with the familiar downbeat songs of betrayal, suicide and depression, helplessness and painful relationships. It railed even more vociferously against fame and the star-making establishment. On some tracks, it veered toward heavy metal. Yet there were also signs that the band was lightening up—well, maybe goofing off is a better description.

The bookends of *Vitalogy*, "Nothingman" and "Better Man," are Pearl Jam's relationship songs—as they've observed and experienced them (which you just know isn't going to feel good). The slow, yearning "Nothingman" is about betrayal, failed love, and empty dreams. According to Eddie, "It's about someone who screwed up a relationship. The idea is that if you love someone, and they love you, don't screw it up, because you are left with less than nothing."

"Better Man," in a sense, is the flip side to "Go" (from *Vs.*). In the hard-driving latter, the male abuser rages against a spouse who wants out. "Better Man" is told (acoustically—most of Pearl Jam's female-point-of-view songs are acoustic . . . hmm) from *her* perspective: "She lies . . . and tells herself, she can't find a better man." It's hard to imagine either of those not being influenced by the experiences of Eddie's mother, who stayed with an abusive husband for many years until she found the courage to leave.

At first listen, it sure sounded like "Immortality" was about the death of Kurt Cobain, with its anguished, "Cannot find comfort in this world/some die just to live." But Eddie says no. This song reflected his own delicate state of mind when it was written—before Kurt killed himself. "It's not about Kurt, but about the pressures of someone on a parallel train, for anyone who's overwhelmed by forces beyond his control."

"Corduroy" and "Not for You" are, in a sense, continuations of "Blood" (from *Vs.*)—about how it feels to be a celebrity. Something which, in case anyone hasn't yet realized, isn't a good thing. The lyrics to "Corduroy" are not printed in *Vitalogy*. But in a very Pearl Jam–esque way, there's an X ray of Eddie's teeth in the space where the lyrics might have gone. "My teeth were in bad shape," he explained, "and analogous to my head at the time this song was written. It's about one person's relationship with a million people—and how that one person (who could it be, now?) doesn't want to be 'held in your debt.'"

And then comes "Bugs." No angst, no activist messages here: This one is just plain goofy. Eddie doesn't even sing, but talks it through. And we learn he's got "bugs in my room/bugs in my bed/bugs in the way I feel about you." And he plays . . . accordion! He'd just picked up the used instrument at a thrift shop and was fooling around with it—and the band opted not only to record the silliness, but put it on the album. "We just decided to do something that was fun to listen to and wasn't bombastic, wasn't everything the band had become," was their reasoning.

Vitalogy was launched without benefit of a marketing plan, singles, or videos. Pearl Jam wasn't concerned about sales. "It's just music—what does it matter?"

FUTURE JAM
"It's hard to stay alternative when you're selling a gazillion records."
—a rock critic

Just watch 'em. There's little question that today's biggest alterna band will continue to surprise its fans and foes alike. They've made some unexpected musical alliances: with Neil Young and Neil Diamond alike. The former is considered a forefather of grunge, and partly to pay homage, Pearl Jam has performed—onstage and at the MTV awards—and recorded an album, *Mirror Ball*, with the aging rocker. But they also invited Neil Diamond, the relic from the sequined '60s, onstage with them during a rare concert in Milwaukee in July '95 (in fact, it was a Ticketmaster thing), and Eddie dueted with the schmaltz icon on his golden oldie "Forever in Bluejeans."

Though resolutely antiradio, last year they bought satellite time and hijacked the airwaves for four and a half hours of what they called "Self-Pollution Radio." Along with other Seattle alterna bands like Soundgarden, they played live and goofed off. The show was free to any radio station in the country that wanted to pick it up—hundreds did.

Pearl Jam is famous for its side projects, and has been doing them since *Temple of the Dog*, the 1992 tribute album (with members of Soundgarden) to the late Andrew Wood. No doubt its members will continue to experiment individually outside the confines of the band.

Mike McCready has played with Mad

Season. Stone has a side band called Brad and discovered and produced a new band called Green Apple Quick Step. Eddie has a baby band that plays unannounced and sporadically in towns around the nation; it's called Hovercraft and it features his wife, Beth Leibling. They've played with Foo Fighters and Mike Watt.

Most poignantly perhaps for Pearl Jam is the addition of its newest drummer—who will most definitely be heard on the band's next album. He is none other than ex-Chili Pepper Jack Irons. The very same man who brought Stone's demos to Eddie back in 1991, and who was responsible, more than anyone, for making Pearl Jam jell. "With Jack, we've come full circle," the band says. And so they have. As they said way back when, "just add water and watch Pearl Jam grow." They're continuing to do just that.

PEARL GEMS: THE VEDDER QUOTES

ON MONEY: "Money does absolutely nothing for you, because it only goes so far."

ON FAME: "I get pissed when I see someone's picture everywhere—on the cover of this, the back of that, in ads, in sound bites on TV. I start to hate that person, whether I've heard their music or not. So I've really tried to hold back from doing that stuff. I felt like, I'm gonna be that guy I hate. I'm gonna be an icon that can be joked about—and I'm too sensitive for that kind of stuff."

ON COMMERCIALISM: "I don't want to be the traveling medicine show where we go out and do the song and dance and someone else drops the back of the wagon and starts selling crap. I don't want to use our music to sell anything—or have anyone else sell it."

ON SONGWRITING: "I can write songs that mean something to someone, and express some of those things that other people can't."

WHERE TO WRITE: TEN CLUB, P.O. Box 4570, Seattle, WA 98104.

THE PSYCHEDELIA OF ALTERNATIVE

smashing pumpkins

ABOUT THEIR NAME

"It could have been any vegetable," head pumpkin
Billy Corgan alleges. He actually named the band before
there *was* a band. "It has nothing to do with pumpkins or
Halloween. It just came to me—there's no related story. But I like
the idea of smashing being aggressive as well as . . . wonderful." Bass
player D'Arcy adds, "Smashing is not a verb, it's an adjective. It's not like we
like to smash pumpkins or anything. And we are not amused by pumpkin jokes
anymore."

VIEUPHORIA

Squarely pegged "alternative," Smashing Pumpkins defiantly don't fit in any easy
round holes. The band embraces all sorts of influences and is not afraid to
experiment with a mélange of styles. Their bone-crunching, hard-rocking wall of
sound is only sometimes played against an Eddie Vedder or Courtney Love–type rage;
just as often, vocals lean toward the frail and emotive, set off by quiet melodies.
Within the same song, they're pedal-to-the-metal intense one minute; pretty,
tranquil, and beautiful the next.

"We make our own little brand of music," touts Billy. "I don't think our fans want us
to be like everybody else. Our uniqueness is respected and appreciated." This is a
band without parameters.

Still, nothing they do is haphazard, random, or arbitrary. Everything about
Smashing Pumpkins is deliberate and carefully constructed, from the harnessed chaos
in their music to their androgynous image; to their legendary inter-band cacophony,
which always finds its way into print.

The formula works: A Pumpkin-hungry public has been lapping up their albums at
record speed ever since the band arrived on the scene five years ago. Smashing

Pumpkins is one of the world's biggest and most successful bands of any musical genre.

MUNCH ON THIS: PUMPKIN SEEDS

"Being in a rock band is just an excuse not to get a job."   —Billy Corgan

The seeds of Smashing Pumpkins are planted firmly within the psyche of William Patrick Corgan Jr., born in Chicago in 1967. The band is his creation, it exists for his music; without him it wouldn't be so much just another band, as no band at all. Billy conceives of, composes, and sings the music, all of which comes from his experience, his (scarred, sacred) heart, and (tortured) soul. He also plays lead guitar; it has been rumored that he played all guitar and bass parts on the first two albums.

As a child, Billy Corgan was never considered "cool," and the music he would make later on is both a reaction to that and a reflection of it. "If you know you're never gonna be cool," he has said, "you might as well tell the truth." His parents—journeyman funk/ jazz guitarist William, Sr., and his wife, Martha—divorced when Billy was young. The little boy was sent to live with various relatives, including, for a time, his great-grandmother, then his grandmother, eventually his dad (who wasn't home very much) and stepmother. Apparently, Billy felt unwanted at each stop. "I feel like I was fucked over," he has said, and has bled openly in the

press, asking such rhetorical questions of his parents as: "Why did you have me if you didn't want me? Why did you have me if you weren't going to take care of me?"

As he told *Alternative Press* magazine, "The way I was raised taught me distrust: 'Only believe in yourself, don't ever put faith in anyone else, 'cause they're just going to hurt you or disappoint you.'"

Billy was an outcast among his peers. "My whole life I was told there was something wrong with me, that I was different. All I ever heard was, 'You're a freak, you're different, you're not like everyone else. You're so emotional, so moody.' For years, I've tried to stuff down my feelings as if somehow I was doing something wrong." His hair wasn't right; his clothes were unfashionable; he had a birthmark that went up his entire arm; he was "larger than every kid—I think in second grade, I was probably twice as tall as anybody in my class."

Even the music he listened to was out of favor. While most kids his age were into the mid-'80s power balladry of Journey and Bon Jovi, Billy was heavy into the kind of metal thought to have died with the '70s. "At twelve I was listening to Black Sabbath, Judas Priest. At fifteen, I moved on to Yngwie Malmsteen, I went down that whole bad heavy metal road." Other musical influences included Led Zeppelin, David Bowie, Iggy Pop, and most of all, Jimi Hendrix.

Because Billy's reality was painful, he often escaped into a fantasy world. He dreamed that he'd be famous, but not, at first, as a musician: He had no wish to emulate his estranged father.

All that changed at the age of fourteen, when he first saw (in his friend's basement) an electric guitar. As Billy has told, "It was like a lightbulb going on—it was a Michael Schenker (brand), black and white, flying-V guitar." Billy's friend wasn't particularly adept at it, he was just making noise. Still, to Billy, it was an epiphany: "At that moment, it all made sense—this is what I was supposed to do." And at that moment, too, his escapist fantasy took the shape of a mythological rock God. "I saw it as a means to become one who has no pain."

Once he'd made his decision, Billy became obsessed with the guitar. He carried it everywhere he went. In those days, he equated playing fast with playing well: His aim was to play always at breakneck speed. He never took formal lessons, but did pick up tips from his father in spite of their estrangement. "My father is a really great musician," Billy acknowledges, "so I came from a place that really valued musicianship." William Corgan Sr. taught Billy not so much *how* to play, but "what I should be thinking about and trying to do."

Through his teen years, Billy was in and out of various bands, doing music from one extreme to the other. In the Smashing Pumpkins's video *Vieuphoria*, Billy explained, "I always wanted to be in a rock band, but when I first started, I was afraid to play rock music because it wasn't in vogue."

At eighteen, he quit the midwest for Florida to form his first "real" band.

Because he and the drummer had very distinct birthmarks, they thought to call themselves The Marked. Unfortunately, the only thing they were marked for was oblivion, and after less than a year, that is what they fell into. Billy became disillusioned. "Being in that band taught me everything I'd gotten into music for was total bullshit. The whole sex, drugs, and rock 'n' roll thing. It was shallow."

Returning to Chicago in 1987 and determined to start over, Billy moved back in with his dad. He'd sit in his room for hours, dreaming of the perfect band. "I definitely had it in my mind to form an exact certain kind of band, a band that could play all sorts of different types of music and not be afraid—not be constrained by what was in vogue at the time. I wanted to do loud music and quiet music and just try to put it all together. I also wanted to take the idealism of the bands I liked from the '70s . . . I liked the fact that they were willing to take chances. When I put on a Black Sabbath record, it rattled my bones—I wanted that feeling."

Billy began to scour the local music scene for three other people, each skilled in a different kind of music. "It's a lot easier to say than it is to do," he said he soon found out.

Which is why, no doubt, things did not come together easily or quickly. "Everything I tried to do to assemble a band was an absolute failure," he admitted. In 1987, through a friend, he met with success in the form of James Iha, then studying graphic arts at Loyola University and playing punk rock in a band called Snaketrain. That James did not play guitar very well was immaterial: Billy simply taught him how. More important, James was open to new ideas—Billy's ideas, specifically.

The two of them bumped—literally—into D'Arcy Wretsky on the street outside a club and immediately got into an argument about the merits of the band playing inside. Impressed with her fiery attitude, and the fact that she played bass, Billy invited her into his band. D'Arcy, who was brought up playing classical violin and singing in choir, neatly fit Billy's idea of each member being able to play a different kind of music.

In this most embryonic stage—as a trio with a drum machine—Smashing Pumpkins played its first gig in front of fifty people at Chicago's Avalon Club in 1988. They weren't a smashing success, but did pique the interest of a club owner who offered them another gig—provided they came up with an actual drummer.

The search turned up Jimmy Chamberlin, a veteran of several Chicago outfits, most recently a jazz band called JP & The Cats. He had no experience with alternative, or new wave, or whatever the

Pumpkins were playing—but Billy liked the jazz element that he could bring to the band, and after hearing the trio, Jimmy decided to give it a go.

The mix meshed—musically, at least—and the Pumpkins began to carve out a niche for themselves on the Chicago club scene. On their fourth gig ever, they supported Jane's Addiction.

All of which so far seems to support the myth regarding Smashing Pumpkins: They had it easy; they were quickly elevated to "hot new band on the local scene" status and never had to pay their dues. That perception reads well (and often) but it's inaccurate. In one of Billy's most candid interviews, with *Alternative Press* magazine, he conceded, "We were just viewed as outsiders, and we played as such for a couple years. We rode around in a van for three years, we played for peanuts, we had faith in ourselves when people said, 'stick to your day job.' My own father didn't care."

As many before them had done, they used gig money to finance their own original album-length demo. In 1990, Smashing Pumpkins put out the single "I Am One" on a label they called Limited Potential. Their first supporter was Joe Shanahan, that original Chicago club owner who'd given them their first break. He sent the demo out, blind, to record company Artist & Repertoire scouts.

In the audience at a small club gig in Madison, Wisconsin, was producer Butch Vig, a man who'd later become famous for producing Nirvana's *Nevermind*. Butch took an interest in the Pumpkins and alerted that icon of indie labels, Seattle's legendary Sub Pop. At Butch's recommendation, Sup Pop offered Smashing Pumpkins a coveted spot in their "Single of the Month Club." With Butch, who'd teamed with the Pumpkins from that time on, behind the console and Billy at the songwriting/guitaring helm, "Tristessa," backed with "La Dolly Vita" was released by Sub Pop in March 1991. A bombastic mix of crunch on one side and psychedelia on the other, the single—along with several showcase gigs—led to the band's pursual by alternative-hungry major labels.

Once again, the myth comes in—and once again, it isn't exactly accurate. It appears that Billy and the band displayed a bravado belying their inexperience by rejecting all the big money offers, including one from Sub Pop itself.

Billy has explained, "We could've signed for megabucks, but we chose to take the hard-earned route, because I've seen too many bands lose on that kind of first album deal. I've been to meetings with the major labels, and suddenly, the band was no longer a band, but a 'project,' and the album wasn't an album, it was a product. Music is about excitement, about buzz, the high that comes around it. You don't get that vibe from a major label."

All of which sounds like so much indie pride, but all of which was kind of lip service. For it's true that in 1990, Smashing Pumpkins did sign with the non-major label called Caroline Records. And it's also true that Caroline allowed the band more autonomy over their album than many big-bucks companies might have. "We couldn't put ourselves in a position where we were powerless," Billy has said. He postulated further, "We weren't afraid to go with a smaller label. We wanted the band to have time to kind of breathe and grow up and not instantly become something that MTV's gonna try and shove down your throat."

But it's also true that Caroline was a subsidiary of the powerful, and major, Virgin Records label—and Smashing Pumpkins signed on with the stipulation that after their first album, and *regardless of its success or failure*, the band would move to Virgin. With that safety net, in 1991, they released their first full-length CD.

GISH
"You don't choose to write a song about pain—it just happens." —Billy Corgan

Smashing Pumpkins's first album is named for the silent film actress Lillian Gish because of a story told to Billy by his grandmother. She grew up in a "nowhere" town: One day the great actress's train came through it. The impact of that seemingly insignificant incident on Billy's grandmother made an impact on him. "Somehow that story and how I feel about the record kind of connect in my head. The album is in a lot of ways childlike in its perceptions: As a child you feel isolated in the world. You're trying to filter a world that's obviously more complex."

Gish defined the band's sound—and gave the first broad hint that the Pumpkins were going to be the band Billy had envisioned: One that could not be contained in any neat packaging. A mix of metal and mellow, power and poetry, with sudden and jarring midsong tempo changes, *Gish* was eclectic all right, and garnered very mixed reviews. *Spin* magazine hailed it as "cerebral rock with balls." One journalist tagged it hippie-metal; another gushed that *Gish* was a "sensuous, androgynous delight—an inspiration to everyone who heard it." Less complimentary were those who felt *Gish* was overlong, confusing, and irritating.

Indeed, all ten songs (except for the last, the D'Arcy-led "Daydream") *were* long—nothing under five minutes. Length was one of the few common musical threads. Which, of course, was all part of the plan. "If there was one simple ethic for the band when we started, it was that we could do anything we wanted to and would not be held down or limited by being a rock band," declared Billy.

There were the bombastic songs like that first single, "I Am One," which was powered by waves of feedback and distorted, overdubbed guitar—Billy's Black Sabbath roots showing—as well as "Bury Me," which opens with Steppenwolf's "Born to Be Wild" played backward.

True to Billy's aim that the music would be loud *and* soft, there were tranquil tunes as well. "That's when you feel most exposed," he's espoused. "It's hard to feel vulnerable when you're all cranked up."

In fact, one thing really did tie the ten songs together: Billy's heart-on-his-sleeve account of the pain of his tough childhood. "The best source you have is your own personal problems," he's said. He chose the sacred heart medal on the CD's back cover to symbolize that. "It's a heart bounded by thorns, with a cross coming out in flames. Almost every song on the album deals with those kinds of contradictions, veering between intense hope and anger."

Ironically, since Billy has steadfastly refused to include a lyric sheet to *Gish*, few may really understand exactly what he's referring to. Listening closely to the album doesn't make it much easier. He's only semi-intelligible when he sings, and legend has it that he doesn't even say the words out loud in the studio. He jokes that if people don't know the words to his songs, no one will know if he messes up in concert. But on a more somber note, Billy admits that fear is what keeps him vague. "Only my mother

and I really know what I'm talking about."

Still, die-hard Pumpkinheads sing along and can relate. "I Am One" more than hinted at Billy's childhood longings: "What you want is what you get/and that is nothing/All I ever wanted was everything/All I ever got was shit."

The sad and beautiful "Snail" is Billy's favorite song on the album and one of the few he's felt comfortable explaining. "Snail is about avoiding—not doing—what's better for you, not facing up to the pain." It's a theme that runs through the album, which actually finishes on an optimistic note. "'Window Paine' is about strength," Billy acknowledges. "I always like to deal with strength, recognizing weakness and overcoming it, or accepting weakness and just moving on, instead of dwelling. I spent years under a black cloud, just dwelling on things, not letting go of the pain." The chorus of "Window Paine," "Do what you're gonna do/say what you've gotta say/start today!" reflects Billy's belief that "it's better to push yourself."

BULLY BOY

Pushing himself—and others—turns out to be what Billy Corgan is best known for. The inter-band disharmony that has resulted is as much a part of the Smashing Pumpkins legend as any hit song. Billy has been branded maniacal, tyrannical, a ruler with an iron fist who threatens to fire band members publicly and at will. "The band is my creation, my voice," he has

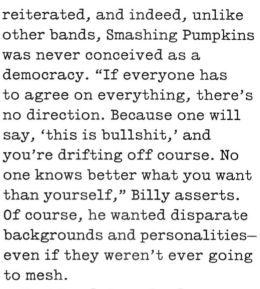

reiterated, and indeed, unlike other bands, Smashing Pumpkins was never conceived as a democracy. "If everyone has to agree on everything, there's no direction. Because one will say, 'this is bullshit,' and you're drifting off course. No one knows better what you want than yourself," Billy asserts. Of course, he wanted disparate backgrounds and personalities— even if they weren't ever going to mesh.

Most bands have leaders, but it's rare to hear them criticizing the others as a bunch of do-nothings who are not interested in the creative process—but should be. "The band pays everybody's bills, the band makes it so they can look groovy," Billy groused to the *Alternative Press* magazine: "They have a freedom, but there's a trade-off to the freedom, and that's responsibility." For many years, Billy didn't believe D'Arcy, James, and Jimmy were taking that responsibility seriously.

Billy has publicly blasted James and D'Arcy for being incompetent and lazy—and Jimmy for his drug dependencies. Further, there's been speculation that Billy scrapped James and D'Arcy's tracks and played all guitar and bass lines himself on *Gish* and *Siamese Dream*. None of the band members has broken their silence so far to refute rumors about who actually contributed what. Yet, a quick read of the liner notes establishes that the artwork on *Gish* is D'Arcy's, and co-writer credit goes to James on *Siamese Dream*'s "Soma" and "Mayonnaise." Both D'Arcy and James have done some lead vocals as well.

The most recent reports have the band getting along much better, and in their video *Vieuphoria*, they even do a skit parodying their dysfunction. Still, somehow, the internal disharmony of the past has worked. Smashing Pumpkins always seem on the verge of collapse, but in the end, the music that comes out speaks volumes and it all comes together.

SIAMESE DREAM
"The point is to let the music be itself. If it doesn't mean anything to you, then it's bullshit."
—Billy Corgan

For a debut album, *Gish* did amazingly well, selling close to a half-million copies. In its wake, Billy should have been on cloud nine—instead, he crashed and suffered a nervous breakdown. He didn't leave his apartment for a month, feeling like, "Life is not worth living. I'm always going to be a freak. Even though the album had sold well and everybody was happy, except me—I'd play these weird insecurity games, feeling like an impostor, that it was an accident I'd sold so many records. I didn't like life, didn't want to continue with the band; didn't care about writing another song."

As suddenly as the melancholy had come on, it broke. Billy "woke up one day and realized my parents were running my life from a distance—like a six-year-old kid looking up to his parents. My fear of love and closeness with people was running my life. And the fear of criticism, the fear that so and so is not going to like you. I suddenly realized that I was never going to be whatever twisted thing I'd created in my head . . . a beautiful, searing, head-thrown-back rock persona— it's just not me. So I decided that I was just going to do the best work that I could do, and stop worrying about what everyone else was gonna think."

Billy summoned the band, and producer Butch, and got to work on their sophomore effort, to be released on Virgin Records.

Unsurprisingly, Billy, who co-produced, had more than a clue as to what he was after. Of *Siamese Dream*, he obliquely explained, "I was trying to get the sound of things like coughing angels, the king and the queen of the prom setting themselves on fire, losers getting laid, high hopes being ripped down and fizzing out." More directly, he also said, "I made the emotional commitment that I wanted to on this record, which is all I cared about." As for the album's name, Billy once explained, "To put it simply, Siamese means connected organically. Dream, we all know what dream means, so a kind of living dream state, an organic connection between people. . . ."

Far more commercial and accessible than *Gish, Siamese Dream* is, according to Billy, "an everything record." But like its predecessor, each cut is unique and unpredictable musically and lyrically. There's the hard-driving ferocity of "Geek USA," and "Quiet"—which is anything but—then suddenly the album takes a turn for the beautiful and dark with the slow, poignant "Mayonnaise."

The pumpkin patch leader felt he was much more open on *Siamese Dream*. "I'm not hiding behind vague, ambiguous images. I'm purposely fleshing myself out a little more," he said, and it does seem to be true. With the help of a lyric sheet (though Virgin only printed 30,000, which is why early pressings of the album include them; later ones do not), there are many more clues to what Billy only alluded to on *Gish*.

Of the popular "Disarm," Billy has said, "it's about my childhood and how I turned into an asshole." Offset by chimes, piano, violin, and cello, the song is a searing trip into his wonder years, *and* an admitted swipe at his parents: "Disarm you with a smile/leave you like they left me here to wither in denial/What's a boy supposed to do?/The killer in me is the killer in you/I'll send this smile over to you."

In "Soma," which features R.E.M.'s Mike Mills on piano, the sense of isolation is resigned and absolute: "All by myself,

that's how I've always felt."

Not every song was a journey through Billy's psyche, however. The guitars-in-overdrive "Cherub Rock" is a swipe at the hypocrisy of the alternative music scene. "Who wants honey/as long as there's some money?" he sings, spitting venom at greed, and the "everyone on the bandwagon" mentality. If Smashing Pumpkins is part of that scene, "Let me out!" is his end-of-the-song plea.

Perhaps the most personal and affecting cut on *Siamese Dream* is the sweet, sad, plaintive "Spaceboy," which was written for Billy's brother, who is autistic. "I have a younger brother who has a rare, genetic chromosomal disorder. He's not a mongoloid, not retarded—but he's definitely different," Billy explained. "The song is a sad commentary about how such people are perceived in the outside world—dismissed as handicapped, they are assumed to be nonfunctional and simple." But Billy didn't mean "Spaceboy" to be depressing, because, "Somebody might listen to it and think, 'Wow, what a beautiful song, it makes me feel good.' It might remind them of someone they love."

Smashing Pumpkins's signature song is "Today," which starts off with a twinkly, bright, melodic feel, and then switches to full-throttle metal, alternating between a loud chorus and hushed verses. A seemingly lighthearted, happy song, "Today" was written at a time when Billy felt anything but: "I felt so low, there's nowhere else to go but up," he describes. The irony is easy to miss, however, as he sings the upbeat chorus: "Today is the greatest day I have ever known."

The day that *Siamese Dream* woke—to rave reviews and better sales, debuting at number 10 on the album charts, and going on to multiplatinum status—had to have been one of the greatest for the entire band. More important, for Billy, "I totally made the record I wanted to make."

The third Smashing Pumpkins album, *Mellon Collie & the Infinite Sadness*, is a twenty-eight-track double CD, which came out in October 1995. The band had been talking it up for several months before its release. As Billy told *Rolling Stone* the previous summer, "In our position, most bands would take a conservative approach, try to repeat our success and do *Siamese Dream II*, but we wanted to do the most nonconservative thing we could. This is an album of 1/3 raw rock, 1/3 spacey stuff, and 1/3 quiet weirdness." Billy further promised some tunes that are "simpler and a lot more direct" than previous Pumpkin offerings; others were meant to be more complicated. "It'll be my 'Wall,'" Billy said, referring to Pink Floyd's seminal effort. "I was born to do this."

As it turned out, most critics and fans agreed with him. A sprawling opus, the double-CD *Mellon Collie* was hailed a big-time rock triumph. Neither a carbon copy of everything they've done before, nor a reach into wholly uncharted territory, *Mellon Collie* is instead a cohesive mix of everything Pumpkins (the deceptively sweet-sounding "Cupid de Locke"), sprinkled with something entirely different, including the classically flavored all-instrumental title tune. There are raging rockers ("Bullet with Butterfly Wings" has been tagged "deranged") as well as tender melodies ("Zero"), plus the lush orchestration found in the powered strings of "Tonight, Tonight."

Although *Mellon Collie* (divided into discs dubbed "Dawn to Dusk" and "Twilight to Starlight") is not a concept album, there are certain themes that run through it. They include familar Billy-laments of broken dreams, blasted love, social dysfunction, and, of course, the old reliable childhood traumas ("I sensed my loss before I even learned to talk" he wails in "To Forgive") and self-loathing, "My reflection/dirty mirror/There's no connection to myself."

Because *Mellon Collie* mixes the purely artistic with the rampantly commercial, the dual disc has moved Pumpkins out of the confines of anyone's definition of alternative and into a much wider arena. Which is kind of ironic, since Billie believes *Mellon Collie* may, in fact, be the group's swan song.

"After this, we'll have exhausted the rock route." The hint is that the band will break up after a tour for the album—but you can never tell where the pieces of a Smashing Pumpkin will land: They are nothing if not unpredictable.

IN THE PUMPKIN PATCH

BILLY BLASTS THE ALTERNATIVE SCENE: "The whole sickness of alternative music is that they're no different from the Paula Abduls of the world. They sit in their little castles and say, 'Well, you're not cool enough, and you're not *this* enough.' It's never based on, 'Is your band good or bad?' It's, 'Are you politically correct? Who do you hang out with?' It's so easy to get caught up in the small, bitchy, bickering world of the music industry and lose sight of the fact that it's still about [this]: you make a record and people like it or they don't like it; they put it on and it makes them feel good, and it makes them love their boyfriend or girlfriend more, or whatever."

BILLY ON GUITAR: "I just look inside myself and try to figure out what I want to say on guitar. Sometimes it means turning it down and playing solo; sometimes it means throwing the guitar across the stage."

BILLY ON LYRICS: "When I first started writing songs, I felt I had to be very honest and I really hated my lyrics because I was uncomfortable with the honesty in them. You could draw nothing out of them because you have to hear only my very specific opinion. Then I went totally the opposite of that, to the point of ambiguity where I didn't even know what the songs were. It eventually worked itself out to where I know what the songs mean, and I think there's enough in there that if you want to connect the dots, you'll come up with something. They're not vacant lyrics and they're not meant to say anything in the sense of me trying to get a message across. The message is there for me—and I found that the most satisfactory route."

MORE ON LYRICS: Hard to get, harder to decipher when you're listening, they are available on the Smashing Pumpkins home page via the Internet. However, the lyrics printed there are not "official," but are as accurate as any.

ABOUT ANDROGYNY: Billy Corgan's voice is almost always referred to as effeminate; physically, he looks as if he barely shaves. While others might play that down, Smashing Pumpkins plays it up: They go further in pushing the androgynous envelope than most other alternative rock outfits. That is part of their credo. "All humans are part male and part female," alleges Billy. "The other side must be explored to gain complete understanding of ourselves and the world we live in. For me, the idea of having a feminine perspective is a willingness to be vulnerable."

PUMPKIN RARITIES: Not on their CDs, the track "Drown" can be found on the sound track to the movie *Singles* (Epic Records), and "Jackie Blue" is on *20 Exclusive Hits of the '70s* (Pravda Records). Additionally, Smashing Pumpkins contributed a track to *No Alternative*, which is part of the Red Hot Organization; money raised goes to AmFAR, American Federation for AIDS Research.

DATE MATES: D'Arcy and James used to be an item; they are no longer.

WHERE TO WRITE: Smashing Pumpkins Fan Club Information, P.O. Box 578010, Chicago, IL 60657.

THE FUTURE OF ALTERNATIVE

The bands in this book represent a small sampling of the branches of the alternative music tree. While each is unique, the nine profiled share what has become alternative's most common characteristics: They are well-known, popular, and sell millions of records. Indeed, a good deal of what once truly was alternative now verges perilously close to what's squarely mainstream.

Originally nurtured by college radio, today more and more Top 40 stations have switched to an alternative, or modern, format. Why? That's where the ratings are. Alternative has its own slice of the ubiquitous MTV pie, called the *Buzz Bin*, as well as its own series, *Alternative Nation*. It has its own contra-concert event, Lollapalooza, and even its own Grammy, MTV Video, and American Music Awards categories.

With all the attention-grabbing hoopla, can alternative retain its edge? As long as there are new bands making new music that moves us, reflects the reality of our lives, and provides an honest and safe harbor for our feelings, there will always be a place for alternative on the radio, in our homes, and in our bones.

An update of this book will most certainly include such newcomer rock rebels as Elastica plus the scruffy teenage trio Silverchair, as well as others with meaty messages: Oasis, Blur, Better Than Ezra, Alanis Morissette, the Nirvana-pedigreed Foo Fighters, Weezer, and countless others now bubbling underground.

As long as the heart of rock 'n' roll is still beating, the power of alternative to grab our guts will remain strong. It may sound completely different ten years from now, but that, after all, is the point.